11 THINGS THAT REQUIRE ZERO TALENT THAT WILL MAKE YOU GREAT

11 Things That Require ZERO Talent
– That Will Make You GREAT
Copyright © 2024 Allistair McCaw

First Edition – November 2024

Published by Allistair McCaw

Allistair McCaw
M

www.AllistairMccaw.com

ISBN: 979-8-9922758-2-7
Library of Congress Cataloging-in-Publication Data

Library of Congress Case
McCaw, Allistair
11 Things That Require ZERO Talent – *That Will Make You GREAT*
Case Number: 1-14206650180 | September, 2024

Category: Motivation, Mindset, Self-Improvement

Author: Allistair McCaw

Editor: Michelle Eyles

Cover Design & Formatting: EliJah Sr. & Jahshua Blyden | www.EliTheBookGuy.com

Published in the United States of America

Disclaimer

Talent v Hard Work:

"Working hard is a very sustainable trait, a part of your character. If you don't have that, at some point, the talent does wear off. Guys who were ahead of me were always way more gifted than me. I had to make up a lot of ground to catch them."
– Tom Brady, NFL 7x Super Bowl winner

"I wasn't born with incredible talent. Fortunately, I learned that passion, purpose and being great at something doesn't arrive with your DNA. They are things you can cultivate and develop over time."
– Ann Hiatt, Executive Business Partner for Jeff Bezos

"Every single successful person who has achieved great things - they've all failed more times than they'll be able to remember. That's how they become great. No one has been great from the beginning. Failure is 100% necessary for greatness."
– Lewis Hamilton, Multiple Formula One World Champion

"You can be the smartest person in the world. You can have more skill than anyone. But there's one skill that few people talk about and if you don't have it, regardless of what you do in life, you're not going to succeed - A work ethic. Hard work is a skill."
– Jerry West, 3x Basketball Hall of Famer

"Anything is possible, and I believe you can train for anything. There's nothing you can't do. You might not become the best in the world at something, but you can be a lot better than you are at anything if you are willing to put the time into learning."
– Rick Rubin, Co-Founder
of Def Jam Recordings

"There's no talent here, this is hard work. This is an obsession. Talent does not exist; we are all equals as human beings. You could be anyone if you put in the time. You will reach the top, and that's that. I am not talented.
I am obsessed."
– Conor McGregor, Former UFC Champion

"Talent is cheaper than table salt. What separates the talented individual from the successful one is a lot of hard work."
– Stephen King, Best Selling Author

"People don't understand that when I grew up, I was never the most talented... the only thing I had was my work ethic, and that's been what has gotten me this far."
– Tiger Woods, Professional Golfer

"Hunger is the only differentiation in people; it's not talent."
– Tony Robbins, Motivational Speaker

"The greats are constructions of their own effort over the years, reversals, mistakes. Champions aren't born.
They are made."
– Sally Jenkins, Sportswriter & Author
of 'The Right Call'

"When I was 14, I honestly couldn't sing and didn't have any talent. I had to work hard at it for years. I believe that you learn everything from failures. And this is the thing that annoys me about the state that the world is in now, is no one talks about failure anymore."
– Ed Sheeran, Musician and Artist

"I don't believe in talent. I'm here because I worked hard my whole life. Without that work, no one would know who I am except my family."
– Ray Allen, NBA Hall of Famer

"My parents taught me the most simple and essential lesson: without a hard work ethic, you have no foundations for anything in sport, business, and indeed, life.
– David Coulthard, Former Formula One Driver

"It takes more than skills to be great. The thing that makes me a step further than others is the obsession and the discipline I have towards the game. Those are my skills"
– Giannis Antetokounmpo, NBA Champion

Contents

11 THINGS THAT REQUIRE ZERO TALENT THAT WILL MAKE YOU GREAT

ALLISTAIR McCAW

Everything in life
is a skill.

And everything that
is a skill,
we can learn.

— Allistair McCaw

INTRODUCTION

N o one is born great. No one is born a Champion. Greatness is not reserved for the most talented or those with an above average IQ. Greatness is a choice. This book is aimed at helping you realize that becoming great at something doesn't require any special gifts, but rather about maximizing the things that require zero talent.

The term *'talent'* refers to an individual's special ability or expertise at mastering skills. It's not something you're born with, but rather something learned through practice. Talent is determined far less by our genetics, and more through our actions.

- Tiger Woods was not born a natural golfer. From the age of 3, he dedicated his life to mastering his craft.

- Vanessa Mae was not born a natural violinist. She spent many years learning how to play the violin until she reached a world-class level.

- Taylor Swift was not born a natural singer and performer. Taylor admits growing up she wasn't the most talented and had to endure many struggles along the way.

- Carlos Alcaraz was not born a natural tennis player. He spent years hitting thousands of tennis balls under the relentless Spanish sun.

What is the commonality among all these high performers? A strong hunger to succeed and a willingness to work hard.

Over the years, I've discovered that successful people are no more talented than others. In fact, science tells us, we are born with very few natural talents and skills. The difference lies in those who are willing to do the things required to be great.

This book is about becoming great at the things that require **Zero Talent.** Having spent over 30 years working with, and being surrounded by, some of the World's best performers, I have seen with my own eyes what it takes to reach the top.

The goal and purpose of this book is simple: To empower you with the belief and mindset that greatness is not reserved for only the special few. It's available to whoever is willing to work for it. Greatness is not about talent. Greatness is about effort.

Throughout these pages, you will discover that everything you need is within you. You will discover and learn that greatness is born not of any innate ability, but out of practice and repetition. If you are willing to do the work, you can make yourself great.

Let's Get Started!

CHAPTER 1

THE RIGHT ATTITUDE

N o matter what field you're in, or what goals you are pursuing, without the right attitude you will always fall short of producing your best work.

This book is about creating excellence and discovering your greatness. It's not about how much talent you have, but more about the attitude and mentality you show up with each day.

Your attitude is where everything starts.
It is your mission control.

You may be talented and possess natural ability but:

- without the **right attitude**, you will never be able to reach your full potential or achieve your best results

- without the **right attitude**, the standard of your work and the quality of your habits will be hindered

- without the **right attitude**, you won't be coachable to advance your skills in order to become your best

- without the **right attitude**, your level of discipline and consistency will falter

One of the most important decisions you will make in life is the attitude you choose. With the right one, anything is possible.

"Attitude is the little thing that makes a big difference."

– Winston Churchill

To create something both meaningful and impactful, you must have the right mindset. Aiming for excellence in your life requires exactly this. Let's face it, it's easy to have the right attitude when everything is going to plan. However, what happens when difficult challenges, adversity, and obstacles appear in front of you? Do you still have the right attitude to overcome them? That is truly the ultimate test.

Know that your success is based on your choice of attitude and how hard you are willing to work on your skills. Just like the clothes you choose to put on that day, or the breakfast you decide to eat, your attitude is a choice.

If you want to change your life, start by changing your mindset and attitude. You are the only person who can do this. Changing this is the ultimate game changer.

Excellence is an attitude.

Success is a combination of both skill and mindset. While having the right skills is important, it's your attitude that really determines your overall success.

When it comes to challenges and adversity, one of the main differences I've discovered between the great and average performers is that great ones can maintain the right mindset and attitude when things get challenging. When it comes to adversity and the average performers, that's when the complaining, blaming and excuses arise. They see problems instead of solutions. They revert to a victim mentality.

You can't expect an A+ performance with a B- attitude.

With the right attitude, you can focus on solutions quicker. With the wrong attitude, you focus on the problems. The difference between successful and unsuccessful people is how they deal with problems and challenges.

The truth is, you might not be able to control what happens to you, but you can control how you respond to it. Eleanor Roosevelt said: *"You can often change your circumstances by changing your attitude."*

Developing the right attitude is about taking full ownership and responsibility of your life. That's why it's vital to focus your energy on the things you can control, like your thoughts, actions, and behaviors.

You are the Captain and CEO of your life. Positive people, and those with the right attitude, still have negative thoughts and feelings. The difference is based on how quickly they can recognize and replace them positively. In other words, awareness is the key to changing your attitude.

You are responsible for the attitude you choose each day. I'm just like anyone else. I too can sometimes wake up feeling lazy or unmotivated. We all get these feelings from time to time. But that's exactly what they are - feelings. I have become more aware when my attitude is poor and try to change it as quickly as I can.

Stick to the plan, not your mood.

I may write books on positivity, mindset, leadership etc. but like you, I also need motivation. One of the habits I've built over time is the habit of gratitude. Instead of waking up and letting my feelings control me, I choose to take control of my feelings. I do this by first thinking of two things I'm grateful for each morning.

I'm a firm believer that starting your day in the best possible way gives me a distinct advantage. By doing this, I am taking control of my feelings and choice of attitude.

The one commonality I've discovered in all my years of working with some of the most successful people is that despite what life throws at them, they chose the right attitude. Jurgen Klopp, the former Liverpool Football Coach once said: "If you don't limit yourself with bad thoughts, you can fly."

If you want to change your results, start by changing your attitude.

In Chapter 32 of my book, *Mindset is your Superpower*, I talk about the differences between a victim and victor mentality. The mentality and outlook you choose in life has everything to do with your attitude. If you have a poor attitude, you will always feel like you are the victim. You will feel that life is unfair, and you are unlucky.

By flipping this and having the right attitude, you will always choose the victor mentality. You are fueled by life's challenges; you feel more optimistic, take ownership, and see obstacles and difficulties as opportunities.

You can't expect to have a winning mindset if you're living with a victim mentality.

I've worked with over 50 Olympians and hundreds of world-class athletes throughout my career. All of them possessed the skills and abilities to perform at the highest level in their chosen sports. What I realized in being so close to these high performers was that when things didn't go so well for them when competing, they didn't cave or crumble. They didn't play the victim or revert to excuse-making or complaining. They instead choose to maintain a victor mindset and adopt the right attitude.

Hall of Famer Football Coach Tony Dungy said: *"Be positive. Your mind is more powerful than you think. What is down in the well comes up in the bucket. Fill yourself with positive things."*

Having the right attitude doesn't mean ignoring your problems or pretending they don't exist. It simply means you can handle them with a clearer and more positive frame of mind, which helps you overcome them quicker.

In the words of Thomas Jefferson: *"Nothing can stop the man with the right mental attitude from achieving his goal; nothing on earth can help the man with the wrong mental attitude."*

In life, you have a choice. You can choose to face your challenges with a positive attitude, or you can ignore them and hope they just disappear. For the record, 'hope' is not a strategy!

"Life is 10% what happens to me and
90% of how I react to it."

– Charles R Swindoll.

With the right attitude, anything is possible.

You and I have a choice every single day. That choice is the attitude and mindset we choose. We cannot change our past circumstances. We cannot control other people or change their opinion of us. However, we can control our attitude and how we choose to think.

John Mitchell once said: *"Our attitude towards life determines life's attitude towards us."* This statement is so true. Life is like a mirror. What we see is a reflection of ourselves. Your mind is a powerful thing. If you allow yourself to keep a positive state of mind, your attitude will follow.

Life can throw many things at you. We don't always have the luxury of choosing the hand we are dealt with. However, people who choose to adopt the right attitude when things get challenging build what we term 'grit.'

Grit can be described as an *act of perseverance.* To persevere means to stick with it; and continue working hard even after experiencing difficulty or failure. Grit is needed to endure uncomfortable challenges. It is about choosing to persevere with something for the longer-term. It is the ability to persist in something you feel connected and passionate about despite challenges that may occur. Grit provides direction, discipline, and commitment. (more about this in Chapter 10).

You might not be responsible for everything that happens to you, but you are responsible for how you react to it.

The right attitude is about controlling the controllables and letting go of what you can't.

With the right attitude you:
- Look for the good in things and others
- Face challenges head on
- Focus on the future
- Embrace challenges and obstacles
- See solutions instead of problems
- Project a good energy and vibe
- Attract opportunities and open doors
- Don't allow negative thoughts to linger

Note: All the above are choices that require zero talent.

You can tell a lot about a person by observing their attitude and demeanor, especially when things don't go their way or as planned. Having the right attitude is essential in not allowing circumstances to affect where you're headed in life.

I've learned that having the right attitude will open more doors and provide you with a multitude of opportunities. I've witnessed this on so many occasions. People climb the ladder of success by having a positive energy and vibe. I've seen people get promoted above more experienced or better qualified people because of their character and attitude. Character always beats skills.

Talent might get you in the door,
but it's your attitude and work ethic that determines
how long you stay there.

When you have these two qualities (the right attitude and a good work ethic), it lands you in places where good luck can find you. Your attitude becomes your reputation and vibe. When you enter a room, you automatically bring an energy into that room - good or bad. When you have a good vibe, you become a people magnet.

When you enter a room, what energy do you bring?

A poor vibe or energy will repel people. *"Your energy introduces you before you even speak."* Your vibe speaks volumes louder than any words could ever speak.

It's impossible to have a good attitude and exude a poor energy at the same time. Just like it's impossible to be grateful and miserable at the same time. A good attitude fuels your energy and effort levels. When you have a poor attitude, your energy depletes. You doubt more. You exude poor body language. You stop giving 100%. You begin to accept average. A poor attitude is like a flat tire. You won't get anywhere until you change it.

Your attitude determines your effort level
Poor attitude = Poor energy
Good attitude = Good energy

Having the right attitude means staying optimistic and positive when things aren't going the way you want, or as fast as you would prefer. Scott Hamilton said: *"The only disability in life is a bad attitude."* By making the decision to adopt the right attitude and mindset, you are not guaranteed success, but you will have the best chance of succeeding.

"A positive attitude may not solve all our problems but that is the only option we have if we want to get out of problems."

– Subodh Gupta

I've also learned that Champions and high performers are serial optimists. They always believe in the best possible outcomes, no matter what the odds are against them. The outcome might not always be the preferred one, but that doesn't stop their belief.

The right attitude doesn't require any special talent - only a choice.

How you use your mind influences your outlook. If you've trained your mind to look for what's good in every situation, you have a much better chance of having the right attitude, no matter what happens. The right attitude also involves looking for the 'good' in people and things.

Who you surround yourself with greatly influences you. It's important to surround yourself with people who adopt a winning mentality. They are positive influencers. Expand your circle to include people who are further ahead in their personal and professional development than you are. These people will help mentor and inspire your journey.

It's vital to protect your energy at all costs and avoid negativity. Therefore, you should make a conscious effort to avoid people whom I like to call, *"Energy Suckers."* Additionally, you can't expect to grow if you choose to hang out with people who aren't investing in their own growth.

Energy Suckers will suck all the positivity
and life out of you.
Avoid them at all costs.

When it comes to protecting your energy, another thing I suggest is to avoid watching the news and following negative and toxic social media accounts. Avoid getting into discussions focused on religion and politics. Make it your goal to avoid anything that isn't contributing to your energy, happiness, and wellbeing.

Nobody likes to fail, but when it occurs, the best performers have adopted a mindset that every time they fail, they are a step closer to success. They embrace the difficult days with the right attitude. Failure helps pave their way to success.

How you respond to something that is uncomfortable
has everything to do with your attitude.

We just have to look at individuals such as Olympic gold medalist in Gymnastics, Gabby Douglas, or Basketball legend, Michael Jordan, to see what a winner's attitude looks and sounds like. When it comes to dealing with the more difficult days, Douglas said: *"The hard days are the best because that's when Champions are made."* Additionally, when challenged and put under pressure, Basketball legend Michael Jordan said: *"My attitude is that if you push me towards a weakness, I will turn that weakness into a strength."*

When an individual with the right attitude is presented with something difficult, they think to themselves, *"This is a great challenge."* They don't play the victim and say, *"Why me?"* Instead, they say, *"Try me."*

Instead of saying "Why me?" say "Try me!"

On the flip side, when someone with a negative or pessimistic attitude is presented with the same uncomfortable challenge, they think, *"This is too difficult. Maybe this isn't for me."*

Which one are you?

"It's not about what happens to you, it's about how you perceive what happens to you. Attitude is everything."

– Wayne Dyer

Champions always find a way. No matter the challenge, they adapt and thrive. The key reason for this? Their choice of attitude.

Whilst on the subject of *"Champions"*, I think it's important to address my definition of what a Champion is:

A Champion is not someone who wins all the time. A Champion is someone who gives everything they've got to win. A Champion is someone who brings the right attitude and effort regardless of how they feel. A Champion is someone who competes with their heart and their head. A Champion always finds a way.

<u>Important notice to all the athletes out there</u>: When you bring the right energy and attitude, you make it extremely difficult for your coach <u>not</u> to select you. The mindset you choose daily will determine your future results. Even with a lesser skillset, but a good attitude, you increase your value in a team. With the wrong one, you make it easy for your coach to overlook you.

***The right attitude can turn a non-starter into a starter
and a Challenger into a Champion.***

The truth is, everyone can adopt the right attitude and a more positive mental outlook towards life. It requires no special talent or gift. While it doesn't always guarantee success, it does certainly increase the chances of it.

Jay Wright said: *"Your attitude is your greatest characteristic. You don't get to control your intelligence, your size, or your God given talents. What you control though, is your attitude. We all can have a positive attitude."*

***Consistency in your attitude, habits and discipline are
the building blocks to success.***

Your attitude affects everything. If you're an athlete, a poor attitude affects your energy. Your energy affects your body language. Your body language affects your performance. It has a domino effect. Everything eventually breaks down. When your opponent sees this, it gives them the motivation to kick your butt.

The opposite is true as well. With the right attitude, your energy and performance increases. Your body language becomes more commanding and self-assured.

You have an aura of confidence. Your opponent begins to doubt.

Good Attitude = High Performance

Poor Attitude = Low Performance

Let's be clear on one thing: Greatness cannot happen without having the right attitude. Excellence cannot happen without having the right energy. Your choice of attitude and energy are what ultimately determine your outcomes and results.

The positive point to keep in mind is that your attitude is within your control and requires no special talent. Only a choice.

Talent might
make you good,
but it's your attitude and
work ethic that will
make you great.

– Allistair McCaw

CHAPTER 2

HUNGER TO SUCCEED

Growing up as a child in South Africa, I had aspirations of becoming a professional tennis player one day. I would spend my days dreaming of playing at Wimbledon and the US Open. This vision would be the first thing I would think about each morning and the last thing before going to bed.

This passion and hunger to succeed would drive me to practice hard every day, come rain or shine. I would spend hours upon hours hitting the ball against the wall of my local club until it was dark. I was self-driven and never relied on my parents or anyone else for motivation or the desire to work hard; that drive came from within.

Be positive. Be ambitious. Be driven.

When you have a deep hunger to succeed, you are internally driven and self-motivated. I was obsessed with reaching my goals and dreams. Fast forward to today, I've learned from observing high performers that being self-driven and having a hunger, are prerequisites to achieving success.

So often I hear people say how badly they want to succeed but their actions, behaviors, and habits don't align with their goals and ambitions. Everyone wants to be successful in one way or another, but the truth is, not many are willing to put in the required work, time, and effort. (See more about this in Chapter 4: *'High Work Ethic'*)

How hard are you willing to work for it?

The idea of being great at something sounds appealing, but the long hours, sacrifices and failures it takes to get there is - well - maybe not as appealing. The most successful people I've encountered in my life, be it in sports, business, or another field, are willing to do what others aren't. They have a different approach and mentality when it comes to doing the work that is required.

It's not what you're capable of doing.
It's what you're willing to do.

Those who are hungry to succeed are willing to:
- work longer
- work harder

- do extra
- outwork others
- work through adversity

When striving for success, you need to be willing to give up something to get something. When pursuing excellence, there will always be life imbalances. It's impossible to have balance when it requires you to spend more time on one thing over another. Priorities create these. The 'great ones' understand this.

How badly do you want to succeed?

English Sport Psychologist and former Basketball coach, Bill Beswick said: *"You've got to ask yourself; how badly do you want it? Because you are going to have to pay a price to be the best. You've got to be willing to work harder, you've got to commit more, you must take more responsibility, you must deal with more ups and downs. It's about how much you are willing to suffer."*

During my lifetime, I've met so many people who had the right skills, experience, and knowledge to succeed, but they weren't willing to put in the hard yards.

Everyone wants to eat, but few are willing to hunt.

When playing sports in school, I remember some of the more talented kids were always the first picks when it came to selecting teams. However, what I noticed as we grew older was that many of them didn't progress and develop as much as time progressed, and they eventually lost interest and fell away.

The ones who struggled more in the beginning stages were the ones who tended to work harder on their game skills. They seemed more engaged when it came to learning. When these kids noticed their progress, it motivated them to keep practicing, and it fueled their hunger to work even harder. They had a more growth-minded approach.

I learned that early success as an athlete could actually be a great disadvantage. The main reasons being that the more talented kids hadn't learned how to fail enough and had inherited a fixed mindset. This influenced the belief they had about themselves and their skills.

A fixed mindset will always hold you back from becoming your best.

I'm sure you've heard the saying..."*Follow your passion and you will be successful.*" I would say this statement is only half true. The truth is: You need more than passion to succeed.

Lots of people talk about passion and how it's the key to becoming successful, but those who have achieved something of significance know that passion alone isn't enough. Together with passion, you need to have a hunger to succeed and a relentless work ethic.

To achieve success, you've got to want it badly. You've got to learn to embrace the journey - the good and the bad. You've got to be willing to overcome the challenges and difficulties along the way. You've got to be willing to put in the hard work.

> **When you are committed to something,**
> **you accept no excuses, only results.**

When you have a passion, you are "interested" and enjoy spending time doing whatever it is. When you have a hunger to succeed, you are committed and 100% invested. You are willing to do what it takes to attain your goals and won't let anything get in your way.

It kind of goes something like this...

When you are interested, you do it when convenient.
When you are hungry, you do whatever it takes.

When you are interested, you find an excuse.
When you are hungry, you find a way.

When you are interested, you do it occasionally.
When you are hungry, you do it consistently.

When you are interested, you go in and out of motivation.
When you are hungry, you stay disciplined.

Make no mistake, having a passion is important but this alone isn't enough to succeed. Passion won't be enough to get you through the tougher days.

No one can give you passion or hunger -
That comes from you.

A hunger to succeed comes from within. It's an internal motivation. You can't give another person hunger. It has to come from the individual themself.

"You can take the horse to water,
but you can't make it drink."

Much the same as you can take little Johnny to baseball practice, but if little Johnny doesn't like baseball, and doesn't want to be there, he won't get very far. In other words, you can't make little Johnny hungry to succeed in baseball, or anything else for that matter.

If you lack the hunger to succeed, it's virtually impossible to become the best you can be. The gap between where you are now and where you could - or should be - is determined by your hunger, self-discipline, and self-drive. If you are not committed, you easily give yourself over to other distractions.

Motivational speaker and author, Les Brown said: *"Wanting something is not enough. You must be hungry for it. Your motivation must be absolutely compelling in order to overcome the obstacles that will invariably come your way."*

Purpose outlasts motivation.

Someone who has achieved success, and gone through obstacles to get there, often found a greater reason for why they did it. Their purpose and *why* was strong enough. Having a powerful enough *why* will provide you with the necessary *how*. Purpose, not talent, can be your greatest asset.

Let your hunger for success be stronger than your fear of failure.

Actor Steve Carell, better known to many as Michael Scott on the American sitcom, *'The Office,'* was once the neighborhood mailman in a small town in Massachusetts.

In an interview, Carell stated that it was the hardest job he's ever had, and he even had to use his own car for the gig. He said: *"I think only the really senior delivery people had the official trucks, so I had to use my Toyota, which had a bench seat. I would sit in the passenger seat and deliver the mail out the right side."*

Carell was hungry to succeed as an actor and was turned down for many roles over a period of 15 years. He endured rejection and failure but kept believing in his abilities. He didn't find widespread fame until his early 40's when he landed the role of Michael Scott in *'The Office.'*

When you are hungry,
you are willing to do whatever it takes.

I remember a conversation I had with the Performance Coach of Formula One World Champion, Max Verstappen. It was November 2023, and I asked him over breakfast on the morning of the final race in Abu Dhabi what made Max so special?

He answered that Max was self-driven and had a relentless mindset when it comes to winning. Even though he had already won the 2023 Championship a few races before the end of the season, he still wanted to win every single time he went out on the track. Max was so hungry to succeed that it didn't matter to him if it was only a pre-season testing session, a practice lap, a qualifying session, or the actual race. Max wanted to win everything and anything.

Max's strength was a passion to compete alongside a relentless hunger to succeed. Max hated losing more than he loved winning. It's what defines a Champion's mindset.

A weak mindset can never drive you to do the things required to become a highly successful person in life. Nothing will stop the person who wants it most.

You can tell when someone is hungry for success without them saying a word. Let's take an athlete for example. You'll see what time they get to practice. You'll see how they prepare. You'll see how they spend their time. You'll see where their energy goes. They're focused and locked in. They're always wanting to learn. They ask a lot of questions. They are curious.

When you are hungry to succeed, you are obsessed.

Many great athletes have overcome adversity during their lives and careers. These adversities have stimulated their hunger to succeed. The following examples below are individuals that have directed their energy and habits around achieving their goals and dreams:

- Eight-time Olympic gold medalist, Usain Bolt, was born with scoliosis - a condition that causes an abnormal curvature of the spine. Many doubted whether he could become a successful athlete, but the Jamaican speed merchant persevered and went on to break World records in the 100m and 200m sprints.

- Professional Hawaiian Surfer, Bethany Hamilton, lost her left arm in a shark attack when she was just 13 years old. Despite this traumatic event and the physical challenges of surfing with one arm, she was determined to reach the top of the sport and returned to become a Professional Surfer. Her hunger to succeed and determination have inspired millions around the world.

- The very first African-American to play in Major League Baseball, Jackie Robinson, faced intense racism and discrimination. Despite these challenges, he remained focused on his game and went on to have a stellar career, breaking the color barrier and changing the face of baseball forever. Robinson's courage and determination paved the way for countless athletes of color to pursue their dreams in professional sports.

Stay hungry. Stay humble. Always be hustling.

I once asked an American Field Hockey College Coach what she looked for when recruiting a new player. Interestingly, it wasn't talent, size, speed, or strength. The first thing she looked for in a player was hunger – a hunger to compete!

She believed that without this trait, the rest didn't matter. She looked for players who had a chip on their shoulders. Not a negative attitude, but rather something to prove. The Coach went on to add that she wanted these players to use past hurt or rejection as a positive influence and motivation moving forwards. She also said that this kind of hunger and motivation provided her with a level of loyalty that other coaches might have bypassed.

You can have the most talented player on the field, but if they don't have a hunger to work hard and succeed, it's pointless.

It's no coincidence that those who have achieved greatness have been obsessed with improvement. Les Brown said: *"The people who want to step into their greatness are hungry!"* They are not satisfied with anything less than their best effort.

When you're hungry for success, you think about it all the time. It drives you to work hard. You are obsessed. Former UFC Fighter, Conor McGregor, said: *"There's no talent here, this is hard work. This is an obsession. Talent does not exist; we are all equals as human beings. You could be anyone if you put in the time. You will reach the top, and that's that. I am not talented. I am obsessed."*

Over the long term, you won't succeed in something if you aren't passionate enough about it and 100% invested.

Success comes to those who want it most - those who have a desire that drives determination and resilience. This passion differentiates from the rest.

The high performers wake up every day with a purpose and an overwhelming desire to get better. They might not feel motivated all the time but are able to maintain a strong desire to keep improving and edge closer to their goals. Their purpose drives their actions.

Hunger helps you stay focused and invested in reaching your goals. Hunger makes you work harder, longer, smarter, and with more purpose. It is easy to get distracted when your purpose is unclear. However, success is more probable once you have clarity. Having a purpose keeps you focused and hungry.

A focus on excellence is what will fuel your passion and hunger. When you wake up with a desire to be better than the day before, you have a purpose. Tony Robbins, motivational speaker and author, believes: *"Hunger is the ultimate driver. Hunger is the part of you that says I will not stop. I will not give up. Hunger will destroy your fear of failure."*

Strive for success but focus on excellence.

When you focus on the everyday process of excellence and driving higher standards, the efforts will compound into greater long-term results. Remember, that success is an outcome which, most of the time, is an uncontrollable. On the other hand, excellence is about the process, which is controllable. Focus on the process.

While others may be coasting or just satisfied with where they are, the hungry ones are fueled by their desire to make progress. This hunger keeps them focused, especially during the more difficult and challenging times.

Arnold Schwarzenegger said: *"For me, life is continuously being hungry. The meaning of life is not simply to exist, to survive, but to move ahead, to go up, to achieve, to conquer."*

Finding your hunger means deciding what you really want. It's one of the first questions I like to ask a new client: *What do you want?* The second question is: *What do you need in order to achieve this?* Followed by: *Why is this important to you?*

Your *'why'* is the reason and purpose you get up in the morning. Purpose outlasts motivation. You can't keep relying on motivation. Motivation is fleeting. It comes and goes.

Purpose outlasts motivation.

When you really know what you want, you choose discomfort over comfort. The challenging part for most people is the lack of belief that they can have what they want and become the person capable of it.

If you look at athletes like Simone Biles or Lebron James, you don't only see a hunger to succeed, but a greater purpose. They aren't satisfied with just being excellent athletes and winning Championships. They want to leave a legacy beyond that. This is what fuels their hunger to keep coming back time and time again.

When you have a hunger to succeed, you have a stronger purpose.

Finding your greater purpose is not always easy. I recall an interview with the former Formula 1 World Champion, Nico Rosberg. He was asked what the most difficult thing was for him when he retired from the sport. His reply: *"Finding a new purpose."* Many athletes find transitioning from a professional to normal life very challenging.

When you are hungry to achieve success, your behaviors and actions will show that. You don't need to tell others how invested you are as your actions and behaviors shine through. As motivational guru, Tony

Robbins said: *"Hunger is the only differentiation in people; it's not talent."*

You can tell a person who has a hunger to succeed. They have a certain vibe and energy about them. They love to talk about their goals, dreams and direction all the time. They will devour books, follow courses, watch videos, listen to podcasts – anything that builds their skills and gives them a better chance of succeeding.

***Winners like to talk about their dreams and goals.
Losers like to gossip and talk about other people.***

When you are hungry to succeed, you will absorb everything to become the best you can be. You become a scholar. Your hunger drives your personal growth.

Ask anyone who has reached the top of their chosen field, and they will tell you that it takes relentless effort over time to make dreams a reality. The hungry ones are those who aren't afraid to fail. They are obsessed about the details. They persist through obstacles and disappointments. Their hunger fuels their grit.

Dwayne Johnson, also known as "The Rock", said: *"Be humble. Be hungry. And always be the hardest worker in the room."*

It's no accident that the best performers are hungrier and more focused than others. The legendary Brazilian Soccer player, Pele, once said: *"Success is no accident. It is hard work, perseverance, learning, studying, sacrifice and most of all, love of what you are doing or learning to do."*

There are millions of people who want to succeed in their personal and professional lives, but there aren't nearly as many people who are willing to do what it takes to succeed.

My hunger to succeed may have started at a very young age, but for others it can be at any stage of their life. The beautiful thing is that you are never too old to set a new goal or have a new dream. If you are passionate about it, willing to work hard, and it fuels your purpose, your hunger to succeed will drive you forwards.

One of the greatest determiners of success comes from having a purpose and a hunger to succeed.

– Allistair McCaw

CHAPTER 3

SELF-DISCIPLINE

When most of us hear the word 'discipline,' we usually think of it from the perspective of rules and demands. As a child, I viewed freedom and discipline as two opposing concepts. I mean, let's face it, what kid loves discipline, right? Thankfully, throughout the years I learned that discipline was, and is, the path to freedom and success. The more discipline you acquire, the more freedom and empowerment you earn.

No success happens without self-discipline.

Motivational speaker and author, Les Brown once said: *"The fact is, self-discipline is only punishment when imposed by someone else. When you discipline yourself, it's not punishment but empowerment."*

Freedom is closely linked to success. If you were to ask me to define what success looks like, it would be along the lines of having the *freedom to choose.* For example, the freedom to choose how I spend my day and with whom. It reminds me of a quote from the great

Kenyan Marathon Runner, Eliud Kipchoge, who said: *"Only the disciplined ones are purely free in life."*

Discipline gives you more freedom to choose.

From a younger age, your parents were likely the people who instilled discipline in you, but as you get older, you take accountability for your own discipline. From the minute we wake up, we are presented with many choices that involve discipline such as:

- the choice to make your bed or leave it unmade and messy

- the choice to sleep in as opposed to getting up early and having a workout

- the choice to eat a healthy breakfast instead of something less nutritious

- the choice to watch TV over reading a self-improvement book

- the choice of scrolling through social media late at night instead of getting to sleep at a suitable time

- the choice of doing some extra reps after practice instead of packing your gear and heading for home

Choices. Choices. Choices……

"Through self-discipline comes freedom."

– Aristotle

Discipline is choosing between what you want now and what you want most.

A commonality observed in successful people is that they get up early. They also make their own beds. They see this as their first act of discipline for the day. Jocko Willink, a former Navy Seal said: *"Waking up early was the first example I noticed in the SEAL Teams in which discipline was really the difference between being good and being exceptional."*

Discipline molds your character and personality. Anil Kumar Sinha said: *"Respectable character is developed by consistency in self-discipline and control."* The road to success involves discomfort and many potholes. Unfortunately, a lot of people go through life trying to avoid these things, thus limiting their own potential.

Learning to instill self-discipline into your daily schedule is the ability to do difficult or unpleasant things because they are better for your wellbeing in the long run.

Discipline is about getting uncomfortable.

Discipline is inherently uncomfortable, so strengthening your relationship with discomfort is one of the best ways to improve self-discipline. The mindset we choose to adopt is crucial when it comes to this.

"Self-discipline begins with the mastery of your thoughts. If you don't control what you think, you cannot control what you do. Simply, self-discipline allows you to think first and act afterwards."

— Napoleon Hill

Discipline is about choosing hard over easy.

If you want to maximize your talents and achieve your best results, you can start with facing your fears and choosing to stay uncomfortable. Discomfort leads to success. Successful people know this. They understand that reaching the top involves getting uncomfortable. That's why they discipline themselves, and don't need others to do it for them.

The gap between where you want to be and where you are, comes down to your habits and self-discipline.

"By constant self-discipline and self-control, you can develop greatness of character."

— Grenville Kleiser

The best have trained their brain to embrace discomfort. They have disciplined themselves to take the hard way over the easy one. They know that there are no shortcuts anywhere worth going. As Lao Tzu said: *"Mastering others is strength. Mastering yourself is true power."*

You need to be stronger than your excuses.
High performers do what's needed regardless of how
they feel. Their discipline overrides their feelings.

When you develop discipline in your habits and daily routines, you set yourself up for success. It doesn't only determine your level of success but also determines how long you can stay successful for.

Developing self-discipline is about the ability to convince yourself to do something, whether you feel like it or not. Longtime Head Coach of Alabama Football, Nick Saban, explains discipline like this: *"Discipline is knowing what you're supposed to do when you're supposed to do it, the way it's supposed to get done. Do the right thing, the right way at the right time – all the time."*

Motivation might get you going in the beginning,
but it's discipline that keeps you growing.

Don't expect to feel inspired and motivated all the time. That's impossible! Even the best aren't. Teach yourself not to count on motivation, but to count on self-discipline. A great example of someone who believed in discipline over motivation was Basketball legend, Kobe Bryant. When it came to self-discipline and sticking to his training schedule, before each season Kobe would make an agreement with himself. He would refuse to negotiate with himself. The deal was already made in his mind, detailing the training schedule.

Why did Kobe do this? He said it was because when things would get tough, and your body started to bite back at you, you would try to negotiate with yourself, and he wasn't going to collaborate. The deal was already made.

It's about choosing the longer-term goal as opposed to short term gratification.

One way to help you master delaying gratification is to think about where you are now and what you want to achieve in the future. All great things in life come from delayed gratification. Anything worthwhile achieving in life is on the other side of something that's going to be hard. You must be willing to endure what's difficult in order to attain your goals.

I remember speaking to a member of the New Zealand Olympic Rowing team about his preparation for the 2024 Olympics in Paris. He mentioned that every time he had the craving to eat a chocolate bar or bag of potato chips, he'd say to himself: *"Is the decision to eat this taking me closer to my goal or away from it?"* His discipline police were in full force! It was a perfect example of choosing the longer-term goal over short term gratification.

The foundations of achievement come from the small acts of daily discipline consistently performed over a longer period of time. The satisfaction of seeing these incremental gains will provide you with the motivation and inspiration to keep going. **The discipline you enforce today determines the successes you'll enjoy tomorrow.**

Leadership author John Maxwell said: *"Small disciplines repeated with consistency every day lead to great achievements gained slowly over time."*

Champions see self-discipline like a muscle.
The more they train it, the stronger it gets.

Every day we will be challenged and tempted to take the easier path. Sleeping in or hitting the snooze button on a cold chilly morning is extremely tempting but I can assure you, nobody achieved anything of significance by doing this. It's like they say, *'when you snooze, you lose'.*

Former Navy Seal, Jocko Willink said: *"The moment the alarm goes off is the first test; it sets the tone for the rest of the day. The test is not a complex one: when the alarm goes off, do you get out of bed, or do you lie there in comfort and fall back to sleep? If you have the discipline to get out of bed, you win - you pass the test."*

It's YOU vs YOU. Always has been. Always will be.

Motivation is difficult for everyone, including World class athletes and performers. They are just like you and me. They too are, at times, challenged by procrastination and lack of motivation. What overrides their feelings is their purpose and the discipline to do what is needed. A Champion pushes through even the tough times. As the greatest Olympian of our time, Michael Phelps said: *"Champions are willing to do what others won't, and they are willing to stay uncomfortable".*

Self-discipline allows you to put forth the kind of consistent work required to reach your goals. When you have strong self-discipline, you will be prepared to overcome any kind of challenges or obstacles that come your way.

Over time you start to see results, whether it's internal or external, when you consistently practice the habit of showing up. Those results continue to build momentum in many areas of your life. When you have strong self-discipline, you are willing to work on the days where you're not feeling motivated. Discipline helps you compete with focus even when your mind seems to be running all over the place. Discipline will take you to your desired destination regardless of your road.

Discipline will take you places motivation can't.

I remember a conversation I had at an event I was speaking at in London a few years ago. The lady's name was Marta who was once a ballet dancer at a highly acclaimed school in Eastern Europe. She told me that even though she never went on to dance at the very highest level, the skills and self-discipline she had gained from her time as a dancer greatly benefited later in her career and life. All the years of hard work, blisters, and aching muscles molded her into the resilient person she is today.

It's a message I relay to others who have been pursuing a certain area for many years. No matter what level you reach, all those years of hard work will never be for nothing. The discipline, habits and skills you gained will always be transferable to other areas in your life.

Discipline and hard work are the currency of success.

Each act of self-discipline strengthens every other act of self-discipline. When you learn to discipline yourself over a longer period, you begin to build a stronger self-image and your confidence grows. You become more competent in tackling difficult situations. You develop grit and a stronger inner belief.

Building your confidence on talent alone is dangerous. When you do this, you become arrogant. You develop a false sense of who you are. **Confidence is built on discipline, not talent.** When you build your confidence on discipline, on how you prepare, on your character – that's when you become a force to be reckoned with.

The most successful people avoid comfort at all costs. One can only grow if they are willing to become uncomfortable on a regular basis. Stepping outside your comfort zone is supposed to feel uncomfortable because it stretches you. Being uncomfortable is a sign of success, not of failure!

Champions know that a comfort zone is
a no progress zone.

When a former Coach of multiple Olympic Champion Swimmer, Katie Ledecky was asked what the secret to her becoming such a dominant force in the pool was, he said: *"Without a doubt, her ability to get uncomfortable and stay disciplined."*

Ledecky, seen as one of the greatest athletes in America, rises each morning at 4am to get ready for her 5am practice. Come rain or shine, Ledecky has already completed her first lap of many by 5:01am. Her determination, dedication, and discipline over the years has resulted in becoming a Freestyle Champion in the swimming pool over the various distances of 200m, 400m, 800m, and 1500m.

Ledecky's mentality has always been about excellence, but that comes at a cost. William Arthur Ward once said: *"The price of excellence is discipline. The cost of mediocrity is disappointment."*

Excellence and discipline are closely linked.

When it comes to talent and work ethic, actor Ryan Reynolds said: *"I have a discipline that has served me very well in my career and in my personal life... and that's gotten stronger as I've gotten older. I've always felt that if I don't just have a natural knack for it, I will just out-discipline the competition if I have to work harder than anybody else."*

This is why we must focus more on discipline. When we commit to making good habits and holding ourselves accountable, maintaining that focus towards the overall goal becomes easy. It becomes a part of who you are.

It's funny how many things go hand in hand in the world of self-improvement. The more you focus on your discipline, the more your discipline will feed your focus. Developing discipline is a key component of success. When you are disciplined, you are more likely to achieve your goals and potential in life.

Without a doubt, I could not have completed this book without having discipline, especially on the days I didn't feel motivated or inspired. There were 100 other things I could have been doing with my time, but my greater purpose and discipline were able to win over my motivation. I told myself that procrastination cannot and will not succeed.

Small disciplines repeated consistently over time lead to great things in the future. Is it easy? NO! Will it be worth it? Heck YEAH!

Discipline requires no special talent, only a choice.

You don't have to be smarter or faster than the rest. You just have to be more disciplined. Let's be clear:

Self-discipline is not punishment. Self-discipline is what's needed to develop resilience and grit.

"We need to understand the difference between discipline and punishment. Punishment is what you do to someone; discipline is what you do for someone."

– Zig Ziglar

5 Benefits of Strong Discipline:

1. **You Create Good Habits:** With more discipline, it becomes easier to hold yourself accountable and create good habits

2. **You Build More Grit:** With more discipline, you persevere and endure discomfort more. You develop a stronger mindset which increases your self-belief

3. **You Increase Your Focus:** With more discipline, you are able to focus and be more present in the moment. You are not easily distracted

4. **You Increase Your Confidence**: With more discipline, you become more confident in your skills and abilities. You also begin to enjoy the process more

5. **You Learn Skills Faster:** With more discipline, you improve the speed of learning new skills and adapt your approach better. Your effort and

commitment to learning these skills increases your competence

"Once you have commitment, you need the discipline and hard work to get you there."

— Haile Gebrselassie

In his book, *"Mental Efficiency Program for Playing Great Tennis"*, world-famous Tennis Coach, Nick Bollettieri, talks about the importance of self-discipline. Bollettieri, who coached over ten number one players in the world, talks about the importance of self-discipline in our lives, not just from a sports perspective, but outside of sport as well. This involves actions that reflect how you plan your day and manage your time. He explains that you develop better habits and skills by being disciplined. These are essential traits and qualities for anyone who wants to maximize their full potential.

"Discipline is the bridge between goals and accomplishment."

— Jim Rohn

Former Seahawks Head Coach and Super Bowl winner, Pete Carroll, believes that when it comes to performing at the highest level, discipline is the ultimate separator. In his words: *"Once you've created the vision and set the goals, you're on your way. But it's the discipline with which you stick to that vision that allows you to get there. You can't allow yourself to be distracted."*

Carroll believes that it's easy in the beginning when everyone is excited about the journey, but that motivation fades away especially when things get harder. That's when the discipline sets in.

Discipline is what separates the best from the rest.

The goal is to hold yourself responsible to a higher standard than anybody else expects of you. Never excuse yourself. When you instill self-discipline and are harder on yourself, life becomes easier in the future.

Discipline is not
about feeling motivated
every day.

It's about showing up and
putting in the work,
no matter what.

— Allistair McCaw

CHAPTER 4

HIGH WORK ETHIC

n all my living years I have never met a successful or high-achieving individual who was lazy, lacked discipline or didn't want to put in the work.

Success requires a high work ethic, which incorporates a combination of working hard as well as working smart. Many people will immediately think that having a high work ethic is all about rolling your sleeves up and getting your hands dirty, but it's much more than that.

A high work ethic refers to the values, principles, and standards guiding an individual's approach to their work. In other words, it's not only about the amount of work you do, but **HOW** you go about your work.

When asked what was the most important skill a person could have, three-time Basketball Hall of Famer, Jerry West said: *"You can be the smartest person in the world. You can have more skill than anyone. But there's one skill that few people talk about and if you don't have it, regardless of what you do in life, you're not going to succeed - a work ethic. Hard work is a skill."*

Hard work is a skill.

There are so many stories about the work ethic and discipline of the late, great basketball player, Kobe Bryant. I remember a conversation I had with Kobe's former trainer at the LA Lakers. One of things he told me was that Kobe **worked like he had no talent, then would play like he believed he was the best player in the world.** He also mentioned that Kobe would, at times, struggle to be around teammates who didn't give their full effort. In fact, this is a common trend in high performers.

Practice like you're the challenger.
Compete like you're the Champion.

Kobe once said: *"I can't relate to lazy people. We don't speak the same language. I don't understand you. I don't want to understand you. I have nothing in common with lazy people who blame others for their lack of success. Great things come from hard work and perseverance. No excuses."*

A good work ethic isn't just about the work you put in. It's about the attitude you choose while doing it.

A high work ethic involves qualities such as energy, desire, and responsibility. The fact is, if you aren't prepared to do the work... if you aren't willing to endure through the setbacks and failure... you will never achieve your true potential...

People with a high work ethic have a competitive spirit. They don't necessarily have a desire to be better than someone else. They instead love to compete against themselves and the person they were the day before. Their goal is to improve daily.

The goal is simple: Be better every day.

Individuals with a high work ethic are highly sought after by coaches, recruiters, managers, etc. due to their drive for progress. They are characterized as having a willingness to take full ownership of their actions and have a laser-like focus to achieving their goals.

Having discipline in your work ethic is key. For example, if you observe the top athletes when they practice, you will notice how focused and locked in they are. Nothing else matters except what they are doing at that precise moment.

A person with a high work ethic will take responsibility for their actions and outcomes. They don't resort to blaming and complaining when things go wrong. They take ownership of their actions and behaviors. They bring an attitude that increases the energy in the room and indicates a high level of passion for what they do.

KEEP IN MIND:

A **trainer** won't make you **fit**
A **teacher** won't make you **smart**
A **dietician** won't make you **slim**
A **mentor** won't make you **rich**
A **doctor** won't make you **healthy**

At the end of the day, **YOU** are the one who has to take responsibility.

A person with a poor attitude and work ethic brings a spirit that sucks the energy out of an environment. They will show a lack of ambition and desire in what they are doing. They look for every possible shortcut and the quickest way to finish a task. What tends to happen is that it eventually needs to be re-done by someone more responsible and who does it correctly.

Choose the right way over the easy way every time.
Shortcuts will only cost you in the long run.

The legendary UCLA Basketball Coach, John Wooden once said: "If you don't have time to do it right, when will you have time to do it over?" He believed: "There is no substitute for hard work. If you're looking for the easy way, if you're looking for the trick, you might get by for a while, but you will not be developing the talents that lie within you. There is simply no substitute for work."

Like the ten other things mentioned in this book that require zero talent, a high work ethic can be nurtured. It is, however, important to note that it's often a part of an individual's character and overall outlook on life that contributes to results achieved.

How hard you work is a choice.

A great example of someone who worked harder than his peers was NFL legendary quarterback, Tom Brady. Recognized as the GOAT (Greatest of All Time) and now retired from the game, his draft report after the NFL combine (trials), read like this:

Tom Brady's NFL Combine Draft Report:

- Poor build
- Skinny
- Lacks physical stature and strength
- Poor mobility
- Can't drive the ball downfield

- Lacks a strong arm
- Does not throw a really tight spiral
- Gets knocked down easily
- Ran one of the slowest 40 yard times (5.2 sec)

Brady was overlooked by a number of colleges. He wanted to go to UCLA but was turned away at the last minute. Then it was the turn of USC, but they also signed someone else. Brady was described by many college coaches as a tall, gangly kid who looked like he'd never seen a weight room.

Fast forward to 23 seasons later and a record 7 Super Bowl wins from 10 finals appearances, Brady went on to become a future Pro Football Hall of Famer and the best-ever to play the game. In Brady's words: *"Working hard is a very sustainable trait, a part of your character. If you don't have that, at some point, the talent does wear off. Guys who were ahead of me were always way more gifted than me. I had to make up a lot of ground in order to catch them."*

A former New England Patriots teammate of Brady once said: *"None of us on the squad could totally commit as much as Tom did. His work ethic was what set him apart from all the other players in the league. His total commitment, lifestyle, sleep, eat, study, work that he's put into that, it was insane. When I arrived at the Patriots, I thought I worked hard, then I watched what he did and put into it and it was on a whole different level. There's a reason why he's the best there ever was."*

Gold medals aren't made from gold.
They're made from the grind.

While it's important to work hard, it's also important to enjoy the work you are doing. What's the point of putting in all those hours if you aren't enjoying the process? Don't lose the love for what you do. Learn to find joy in the process of becoming.

Mike Rowe, the American television host and narrator also known for his work on the Discovery Channel series, 'Dirty Jobs', said: *"Work ethic is important because unlike intelligence, athleticism, charisma or any other natural attribute, it's a choice."* On this subject, Rowe went on to say: *"Hard work is essential for success, and a key part of getting things done. Everyone deserves to have a great personal life – everyone manages that in their own way – ambitious people find ways to blend and balance the two."*

I am a huge believer that the time you rise in the morning matters. Over the years, I've become aware that the most successful people get up early. On top of that, they have a game plan for their day. They have structure and follow daily routines.

Successful people have a game plan for their day.

George Allen Sr. once said: *"Work hard, stay positive, and get up early. It's the best part of the day."* I wholeheartedly agree with this comment. My high level of productivity before 9am in the morning gives me a huge sense of accomplishment. It sets up a positive start and strong momentum for the day ahead.

I also believe that when you have a high work ethic, you become luckier. Wait, what? Yes, you read correctly. **A high work ethic and good attitude will position you in situations where good luck can find you.**

The South African Golfer, Gary Player was once famously quoted as saying: *"The harder I practice, the luckier I get."* I can relate with this statement as I experienced it in my own athletic career. If I was willing to work harder (and smarter) than my competitors, I would eventually prevail. I learned that when we are achieving our best results, we are usually working harder at improving and getting more consistent. This consistency and momentum also builds confidence.

"Practice creates confidence.
Confidence empowers you."

– Simone Biles

When you know in your heart you've prepared well and put in the hard work, a deep inner confidence is instilled within you. You grow that inner confidence by feeding it with affirming positive self-talk.

Knowing that you've put the hard work in builds your confidence.

One thing that drives me nuts is when people call an elite performer a 'natural' or they're just 'lucky' or 'talented'. They see athletes like Tennis player Coco Gauff, Surfer Caroline Marks, or the actress Blake Lively, and presume they were all just born with all those gifts and talents.

What many don't see are the countless hours these high performers are tirelessly working, trying to perfect their craft away from the public eye. The best in their fields have dedicated years of practice, countless repetition, and a dedication to become the best at what they do.

The truth is, talent doesn't prepare you for the grind. Talent doesn't prepare you for the obstacles and setbacks. It's all about the ability to work hard and grind it out when things don't look like they're going to turn out.

Work hard in silence. Let success be your noise.

Taylor Swift is one such example whose success didn't come overnight. She worked hard for years behind the scenes, performing at small local venues, and sending demos to record labels before she was discovered. Even after Taylor's initial success, she continued to strive for excellence and take risks, such as when she left her former record label to start her own.

Like many other artists, Taylor has faced her fair share of setbacks and challenges. But in her words: *"You need to stay persistent and not give up. Keep working hard and take calculated risks, and don't be afraid to pivot when necessary".*

Hard work and persistence pay off. Maybe not today, maybe not tomorrow. But eventually, it pays off.

I was in Dubai a few years ago for an off-season training camp with a professional athlete. Our next-door neighbor was a certain Swiss guy by the name of Roger Federer. What I remember most about the twenty-time Grand Slam Champion was his tireless work ethic and willingness to be coached. Roger craved feedback and would spend hours discussing the smallest details with his coaches. I observed this for almost 3 weeks and was impressed how meticulous he was in his preparation.

In an interview with Roger, after he'd just retired in 2023, he said: *"Even when I was the Number One player in the World, I would ask myself, "What can I improve? What do I need to change?" Because if you don't do anything, or you just do the same thing over and over again, you stay the same. Staying the same means going backwards. I always needed to find new ways to improve my game."*

Staying the same means you are going backwards.

Anyone who was lucky to see Roger play, will tell you how beautiful and effortless his game looked. South African tennis commentator, Robbie Koening described it as *"a thing of beauty."* Roger wasn't afraid to learn, evolve, and work his hardest – every day.

"There is no way around the hard work. Embrace it. You have to put in the hours because there is always something to improve on."

– Roger Federer

Another great example of someone with an impressive work ethic is Eric Spoelstra, the longtime coach of the Miami Heat Basketball team. Spoelstra started as a backroom video coordinator at the Heat. However, with his enthusiasm, attention to detail, and tireless work ethic, he worked his way to the top and was eventually promoted to the Head Coach position.

Spoelstra's story is a great reminder for all of us to be faithful with the small things because you never know who is watching.

Consistent hard work always pays off. Hard work builds grit. If you want to become great at what you do, you will have to do things that other people aren't willing to do. It's that simple.

A high work ethic is earned, never given.

Here's a little secret: When you consistently pitch up with the right attitude and work ethic, you make it hard for your coach, manager, or boss not to start, select or promote you! Aim to make work ethic one of your strongest qualities. Build a reputation around being known as a grafter.

When it comes to effort, make it a non-negotiable rule for yourself to always give your best. Pride yourself on your effort. Make it part of your reputation and DNA.

James Milner, a professional Footballer who has played for English teams such as Leeds, Manchester City and Liverpool, might not have been the flashiest player on the field, but according to his teammates, had the highest discipline and work ethic. They regarded James as a beacon of reliability who would never let you down – a player who consistently brought his A-game, whether in training or in a match.

Discipline and a high work ethic earns you respect.

During James's time at Liverpool, his Manager, Jurgen Klopp said: *"James is an example to the rest of the team, especially the younger players. Throughout his time here, he always gave 100% effort. He had a relentless work ethic and was someone I could always rely on."*

Habits are also a key component to your level of success. The quality of your habits will determine the quality of your life. If you have a strong work ethic, you'll take the time to cultivate strong habits instead of adopting poor ones.

Never be afraid to do the extra work. The extra work is what eventually separates you from the competition. Don't wait to be asked to do it. With the right mindset, you choose to do the extra work.

The best performers take it upon themselves to do the extra work. Sportswriter and author Sally Jenkins said: *"Michael Phelps was not born with an innate sense to* swim fast. His body was well suited to swim but not much more than any other Olympian. The work is what made him great."

When Michael's mother, Debbie Phelps, was in Beijing, she often had to field questions about her son. Was it his size-14 feet? His extra-long arms? His breakfast regimen? Debbie answered repeatedly: "No - It's his hard work."

Hard work always beats talent when talent doesn't want to work hard.

A lot of people might think that Tiger Woods' success came down to his talent. In reality, what he did was outwork everyone around him. Some might argue it wasn't the healthiest of upbringings due to the workload his father placed upon him at such a young age. Regardless, the point I'd like to make is that his work ethic enabled him to become the greatest golfer in the world.

In Tiger's words: *"People don't understand that when I grew up, I was never the most talented... the only thing I had was my work ethic, and that's been what has gotten me this far."*

In a conversation I had with a trainer at the French League 1 Football Club, PSG, I asked about their star player at that time, Kylian Mbappe. This particular trainer had worked with Kylian for four years. I was curious to know what kind of work ethic the French star Forward had, as when watching him, like Federer, the game just looked so 'natural' for him. He was quick to stop me in my tracks by telling me that Kylian was probably the hardest worker in the entire squad. *"The ultimate professional,"* he said.

"It's no coincidence that Kylian is one of the world's best players. He's always on time, gets his workouts in, does treatment afterwards (as where some other players would leave early). He stays after the normal team practice to work on perfecting his free kicks, set pieces etc. It's not his talent that makes him so good, it's his attitude and work ethic. He always arrives ready to work hard."

No one is born a 'natural.'

No one is born a natural. It's all about practice and repetition. On her journey from performing to a hand full of people in a small dive bar to becoming one of America's best-known comedians, Nikki Glaser had this to say:

"When pursuing comedy or any other skill for that matter, be prepared to suck. You're going

to suck at anything you're a beginner at, don't forget it. And don't think that you're more special. Beyoncé didn't arrive on this planet singing and dancing like that. She worked her tail off and she lost her childhood because she was singing and dancing so much. Everyone seems to think that Beyoncé just showed up and was amazing. Beyonce was so scared that she even created an alter ego when she went on stage".

It's so easy for all of us to presume that someone as successful as Beyonce would have been a natural and, as Nikki said, just came into the world and could perform like that.

Nikki went on to add: *"I love the line in the Taylor Swift song, 'Mirrorball' that says I've never been a natural. All I do is try'. Taylor Swift has never been a natural. So don't convince yourself you're one. You've just got to be willing to put in the work and you've got to be comfortable with being uncomfortable. If I look back at my beginning as a comedian, this is all the advice I needed to hear."*

There are NO LIMITS to what you can achieve.
The only limits are the ones in your MIND.

Having a high work ethic has so many benefits:
- You will gain more confidence
- Others will trust how you carry out a task
- You will see a rise in your productivity
- You will be modeling good values and standards
- You will feel more accomplished
- You will open more doors to opportunities
- You will become 'luckier'
- You will build stamina, focus and persistence
- You earn respect

A strong work ethic should be a non-negotiable for anyone who wants to succeed in their career and personal life. It's the foundation for all future success.

So let me ask you:
How hard are you willing to work?

To be in the top 1% you need to be willing to do what the 99% won't.

– Allistair McCaw

CHAPTER 5

STRONG SELF-BELIEF

S elf-belief is one of the most powerful gifts you can ever give yourself.

You can have all the skills and tools needed to succeed. You can be surrounded by all the right coaches, people and environment. You can even be the hardest worker and the most prepared, but the fact of the matter is this: **if you don't BELIEVE in yourself, you will never achieve your full potential.**

So, what is it that holds people back from believing in themselves more? I believe there are four things that stand in the way of an individual changing their self-belief for the better:

1. an attachment to past self-limiting beliefs

2. a fear of what others think

3. a poor self-image

4. a comparison to others

Most of my work entails working with high performers in a wide range of sectors including the sports industry, education sectors, and the corporate and law enforcement worlds. Regardless of what field they are in, I would say that 80% of the people I've met don't fully embrace the power of self-belief. Isn't that sad?

Competence + Confidence = Success

Having the skills, of course, is an important component of performing well, but what use are these skills if you don't believe in yourself and the work you do?

I've discovered that many people are almost afraid to fully believe in themselves. This can be due to several factors, including a fear of success. But wait, how can one be afraid of succeeding you ask? Don't we all want to succeed? The answer to that question comes from the questions - *'What if I try my best and fail?* and *'What will others think of me?'* Sally Jenkins, Sportswriter and Author of the book, *"The Right Call"* said: *"A lot of people are afraid to win. They are afraid to put it all on the line and risk not being enough."*

Life is too short to play small in this world.

We fear the opinions of others. That's the problem. We then choose to play small and not really go for it.

Do you want to know what one of the biggest regrets people have later in life? They wish they had believed in themselves more. Unfortunately, a lot of people sabotage their own success by not giving it their all. They become their own worst enemy.

Sometimes the best thing you can do to become your best self, is get out of your own way!

Never let any person, any obstacle, any doubt, any fear, or negative voice keep you from becoming who you want to be. Don't become your own biggest enemy. There are enough people waiting in line to do that for you. You are the only person who can decide what and who you become.

If you insist on sabotaging your own efforts, you're choosing (consciously or unconsciously) to hold yourself back. Remember that the mind is an incredibly powerful tool.

Your thoughts hold power.
You become what you think.

Too often, we look at others and compare our self-worth. Comparison will always be a no-win game as we are all uniquely different or we look at our past and use it to determine our future. Both are massive mistakes.

Belief in yourself begins and ends with your mindset. We become what we think and what we believe becomes our reality. You eventually become what you feed your mind.

Many people think you first need to build your confidence before you take the jump. When in fact, you build your confidence by taking the jump. Let's face it, nobody ever learned to drive a parked car.

The 'doing' is what builds your confidence and self-belief.

Do you want to know one of the most disempowering words in the English language? The word *'Can't'.* It is a word that holds you back from achieving your greatest potential. High performers don't allow this word in their vocabulary.

However, there is one golden rule. If you ever are going to use the word *'Can't.'*, instead of saying, *"I can't do this"* change it to, *"I can't do this **yet**."* Like everything else, it all starts with your mindset, with the conversations you have with yourself, and the things you choose to believe.

When we say we can't do something, we are immediately admitting defeat. The goal is to train your brain to add *"yet"* at the end of that phrase. This one little word changes everything.

The word 'can't' should always be followed by the word 'yet.'

Henry Ford famously once said: *"Whether you think you can, or think you can't ... you're right."* This statement emphasizes how much your attitude determines your outcomes. It means that you ultimately manifest either your own success or failure.

Someone who wasn't short of confidence or self-belief was the great Boxer, Muhammad Ali. He was never afraid to speak his mind or let others know he was the greatest. One of his most famous quotes was: *'I am the greatest, I said that even before I knew I was.'*

What Ali understood well was that the more you tell yourself something, the more you will begin to believe it. It's the repetition that instills the belief and thus eventually becomes reality. Ali was also a master in playing mind games with his opponents. Even before they entered the ring, they already believed he was the greatest.

We are limited mostly by what we believe is possible. Belief is the key ingredient to achieving great things. When you believe in yourself, there are very few limits to how far you can go. Without a firm belief in yourself, there is no action, no growth, and no achievement. You will always be holding yourself back from your best results.

High performers visualize their success daily.

Visualization is another powerful method in which to build self-belief. The best performers have visualized what they wanted long before they achieve it. Some have spent years visualizing their biggest goals and dreams. Gymnast Simone Biles is one such person who endorses visualization.

When Serbian Tennis player Novak Djokovic was only 11 years of age, he told a reporter live on television that he would one day be the number one player in the world. He said he would visualize it in his mind every night before going to sleep. Fast forward to today, Novak hasn't only gone on to achieve the most weeks as the world number one tennis player but has also won the most Grand Slam titles by any male player in the history of the sport.

Novak believed he would achieve these goals from a very young age. He saw it in his mind first. Like many other world class athletes and performers, Novak harnessed the power of visualization to help propel himself closer to his dreams and goals.

Another great example of an athlete who used this same technique was the Olympic Swimmer, Michael Phelps. From a young age and up until his very last competition, Michael visualized his races before stepping onto the starting blocks and maintained the end goal of being the first swimmer to touch the wall.

If you are able to see it, work for it, and believe it – you can achieve it!

There's a huge difference between saying *"I think I will"* and *"I know I will."* The difference between those 4 simple words is a game-changer. **Don't just think you will succeed. Believe you will succeed with all your heart.** Keep repeating to yourself over and over until it becomes a deep inner belief. But remember - you still need to put in the work. Words without work are nothing more than just words in the end.

One of the best Basketball players in the NBA is Draymond Green. A three-time NBA All-Star, and a four-time NBA Champion, Green believes that a strong mindset and self-belief are key. In a press conference ahead of the 2019 NBA Finals, Green revealed how important belief is to success.

Green said: *"If you're trying to do something meaningful, if you don't have the mindset that you are the best ever, then you've failed already. So, if you don't have the mindset that you're the best reporter ever, then you already failed. And that has been my mindset since I can remember. That will be my mindset as long as I can remember anything - that I am the best ever at what I do. And every day that I step on the basketball floor I will strive to be that."*

Green went on to add: *"Before you can ever reach anything you have to believe it. You don't just mistakenly become great at something - you probably at one time or another, believed that you could be great at that. And then you worked to get great at that and you reached that greatness. But you don't mistakenly become great and then you start to believe, 'Oh man, I'm great at that!' No, you believed that before, and you worked to get that. So, I always believe that, and I work every day to reach that goal."*

At the core of self-belief is realizing that you – and only you – are the captain of your ship. You are responsible for your own success.

The more self-belief you build, the more it acts as a buffer against self-doubt and fear of failure. It allows you to bounce back from setbacks and learn from your mistakes. When you start believing in yourself, your self-confidence becomes a self-fulfilling prophecy. Like any other skill, self-confidence can be learned, practiced, and mastered.

Belief in yourself doesn't guarantee that you'll win or succeed every time. What it does give you is a far better chance of succeeding. When you believe in yourself, you are more likely to view failures as valuable learning experiences and opportunities. This resilience is essential for long term success because setbacks are an inevitable part of any journey.

A common habit of all high performers is that they focus more on their strengths and what they excel at. This not only feeds their confidence, but also their enjoyment in what they are doing.

Self-awareness leads to self-improvement, which leads to growth. When you shift your attention and focus to recognizing your strengths, you will effortlessly feel more competent and confident. Your strengths are what add value to your personal resume.

Recognizing your strengths and daily wins help build your confidence.

I always like to remind others that confidence is like building a brick wall. When you take the time to recognize all the small wins you make daily, you keep adding bricks to your wall of confidence. The opposite is true as well. When you only recognize the things you haven't done well and beat yourself up about it, you break that wall of confidence down by removing bricks from it.

Multiple Olympic gold medalist and World Swimming Champion, Adam Peaty believes that it's important to applaud yourself from time to time, and that whilst having humility is an aid to an athlete, it is also important to have self-belief and to recognize your achievements.

Self-awareness is key. This is the foundation of a sense of self. It involves recognizing and understanding one's thoughts, feelings and behaviors, and the ability to reflect on one's own experiences and actions. Tennis legend, Billie Jean King said: *"I think self-awareness is probably the most important thing toward being a Champion."*

When NFL Football Coach Pete Carroll was asked what it took to be an elite performer, not only as a coach or athlete, but in life, he said: *"The essence of being as good as you can be is that you have got to figure out who you are. If you don't do the self-discovery, then you don't have the opportunity to be your best because you don't know who you are yet."*

Carroll's words are a reminder that to become your best and have a strong sense of belief and purpose, you must understand what kind of person you are. His belief is that authenticity and self-connection are the keys to discovering greatness and sustaining excellence over time.

> **Belief in oneself and knowing oneself are key paths to achieving excellence.**

Self-belief is about acknowledging your weaknesses, not ignoring or shying away from them. It's about taking ownership of your whole existence and facing it with courage. By developing greater self-awareness, and understanding the factors that limit us, we face our reality, and our mindset begins to shift.

A strong self-belief is about choosing to have a winning attitude. You teach your mind to see the positive opportunity in every experience - negative or positive. People with a strong self-belief have trained their minds to focus on opportunities and the bigger picture. They have learned to deal with rejection.

Your life is no better than your relationship with yourself.

One of the greatest coaches I ever had the opportunity to get to know and work alongside was the great Tennis Coach, Nick Bollettieri. Players from all over the world flocked to Bradenton, Florida where Nick was based, wanting to work with him. Nick's leadership style and approach was all about instilling confidence and self-belief in those he worked with. This was his **SUPERPOWER.**

His method of coaching was all about the power of self-belief and teaching the player to focus on the positive things. He was a genius and master motivator. I witnessed many players walk onto Nick's court who were either suffering from a slump in performance or loss in confidence, only for them to walk off the court taller than the Empire State Building. It was all about **BELIEF**!

Nick didn't necessarily change their game or meddle with their technique. Instead, he transformed their mindsets and made them see what they could become. He empowered them with the self-belief to become Champions. Nick instilled a *never-say-die* attitude into his players and continuously liked to remind them that, *"Champions always find a way to make it happen."*

When you harness the power of self-belief, anything is possible.

On finishing this chapter, I'd like to talk about the importance of your circle. And by that, I mean, those you choose to surround yourself with.

Who you surround yourself with matters more than you think.

A Harvard study looking into why some people succeeded greatly in life found that as much as 99% of success is determined by what they termed *'your reference group.'* Your reference group are the people with whom you habitually associate with. It also found that relationships determine 85% of our happiness or unhappiness.

Who you hang around with matters big time! It influences your habits, mindset, and your future more than you think. Who you associate yourself with plays a big part in your confidence, self-belief, and general wellbeing. That's why it's important to surround yourself with people who support and encourage you.

Surround yourself with winners.
The conversation is different.

Your circle should only include people who are genuinely happy to see you succeed. Those who challenge you to be a better version of yourself. Those who give you the honest truth. When it comes to your circle, focus on quality, not quantity. It's better to have two real friends than twenty false ones.

Stay away from the 'good weather' friends - those who are only there when times are good but disappear when things get tough. Stay away from the energy suckers and vampires. Avoid them at all costs. Avoid those who tell you that you can't do something. They are the ones who fear your success.

Negative influences and people will erode your confidence and chances of success. Choose who you spend your time with wisely. Protect your energy. When you protect your energy, you don't allow for negative people or drama to come into your space. Be mindful of your environment. If you don't do this, your self-belief can be diminished very quickly.

Don't allow outside opinions to define your reality or disrupt your peace of mind.

From today, I encourage you to pay more attention to your inner voice. Replace unhelpful and negative self-talk with positive affirmations that reinforce your self-belief. Don't let the regret of not believing in yourself hold you back from becoming what you were meant to be. Doubt, fear, and lack of belief has killed many a person's dreams. Don't let that be you.

Remind yourself daily what your strengths and past successes are. Make it a habit.

Be optimistic about the future, regardless of where you are right now in your life. This is how you build your wall of confidence and self-belief.

Getting from good to great usually is a matter of self-belief.

– Allistair McCaw

CHAPTER 6

FOCUS

I n the last twenty years, the world has advanced further and faster than it has in the last two centuries. Today we have more distractions than ever. The obvious one, of course, being our smartphones. We have become dependent on them. In fact, did you know that on average, people check their phones 144 times a day?

The ability to focus is a valuable skill that can greatly impact your productivity and success. Studies have shown that staying focused is vital for cognitive performance. In other words, for your brain to do its best work, it needs you to be focused on what you are doing.

Entertainment, social media, and advertising have never been so prevalent. Consider the vast amount of information we are exposed to daily, which is coming to us faster, louder, and brighter than ever before. It begs for our attention and focus. In doing so, our minds are diverted from more important work. As Seneca, the stoic philosopher of ancient Rome once said: *"He who is everywhere is nowhere."*

Focus is the art of what to ignore.

Obtaining excellence can only be achieved when we are able to focus all our attention on what we're doing at this present moment. If we allow distractions to intervene, it's very likely that the quality of our work will suffer from it. In fact, when I sit down to write, I won't have my iPhone in the same room because I know, without a doubt, I'll be distracted.

The author and motivational speaker, Zig Ziglar once said: _"I don't care how much power, brilliance, or energy you have, if you don't harness and focus it on a specific target, and hold it there, you're never going to accomplish as much as your ability warrants."_

Discipline is the capacity to get past distractions.

Focus was something I struggled with at times during my younger years. For example, if I was playing tennis, a bad line call could hinder my concentration and ability to focus on the next play. Additionally, if something was happening outside the court, this took my focus away from the game.

My coach would tell me not to dwell on what went wrong or be distracted by irrelevant things but to focus on the next play. She advised me to stay disciplined and spend my energy on moving forwards. It was great advice that I have passed on to many athletes and clients.

In today's world, the ability to eliminate distractions and focus on a single task has almost become a superpower.

Have you ever watched the Olympic sport of Archery? If you have, you will most likely have noticed the intense focus of an archer. When preparing to take aim and release the arrow, their eyes are deeply fixated on the center of the target, and their bodies are motionless. It doesn't even look like they are breathing!

Whilst working at the United States Olympic Training Center in Chula Vista, California, I decided to stop by the Archery Center and watch a practice session. When observing the athletes, each one had the concentration and focus of an American bald eagle, as if it was swooping in on its prey. After the practice had finished, I asked one of the athletes what it was like to be in such a focused and attentive state. She paused and then answered: *"It takes many years of practice because in the beginning, I couldn't keep my focus for more than ten seconds!"*

She went on to explain herself further by saying: *"When I am in the zone and completely focused, it's almost as if time stands still. Everything slows down including my heart rate. Before I am just about to release the arrow, everything becomes completely silent... until the moment I release it. Then the world kind of 'opens up' again and you are back to reality."* It was really fascinating how she described it to me.

Deep focus is a learned and practiced skill.

Two-time U.S. Women's Chess Champion, Jennifer Shahade, learned how to play chess from her father when she was about five years old. By nine, she was playing in her first tournament, and by high school, Shahade was competing around the world.

When asked for the best tip she could give to younger players, she said: *"Deep focus and deep concentration are the most important skills to develop."*

Asked how she was able to keep her focus, she said: *"I go for walks."* Shahade explained that during a chess tournament you are sitting at a table with your body not moving for hours, but your brain is. That's why, in between games, she likes to go outside for a walk if she can.

Shahade said: *"Inside the room, the moves are racing furiously through your brain. So, it kind of leaves you in this weird state afterwards, where you're tired but your body didn't really move a lot. So, it needs to move to play 'catch up' with the brain in a way, and that's why I like to go for a walk to help me recharge and be able to focus better and not become distracted."*

Starve your distractions, feed your focus.

World class athletes and performers have the ability to cut out distractions and ignore everything else that is going on around them. When you are genuinely focused on something, your mind becomes clear of distractions. Distractions are actions that move us away from what we really want but as the young female Archer explained to me, improving your focus takes practice – *"lots of it"*.

When you watch some of the world's best performers in their field, be it in sports, music or the arts, you will discover they are completely locked into what they are doing at that very moment. They will tell you that when they are in such a focused state, they lose sight of everything else around them. They get *'in the zone.'* Through years of practice, outside distractions are easily resisted or entirely blocked.

Where attention goes, energy flows.

Tennis Champion, Roger Federer describes focus as the most important thing in the world. In his Dartmouth commencement speech in 2024, Federer said: *"When* you are playing a point, it has to be the most important thing in the world. The mindset is crucial - because it frees you to commit to the next point with intensity, clarity and focus".

Many years ago, I was working with the world's best squash player who had won multiple World Championships. What I remember most from our time together was how focused she was whilst practicing.

Her incredible ability to be present and deeply focus in practice was something that greatly benefited her when competing. It reminds me of that great Kobe Bryant quote: *"It's not the number of hours you practice, it's about the number of hours your mind is present during the practice."*

Focus becomes a habit.
The more you practice it, the better it gets.

Like exercising the body, Kobe found that exercising his mind made it a lot easier to center his attention when needed, which turned him into one of the greatest players to ever take the court. Kobe believed that if you could do that every time you step onto the court, you'll get to where you want to be.

Speaking in an interview with the American sports television channel *ESPN*, Kobe once said: *"It's all about focus. I don't care who you are, where you're from, that doesn't matter. It's about having a focus and having a purpose. You wake up every single day to get better than you were yesterday. Doesn't matter what you are, a basketball player, hockey player, golfer, painter, etc. It's about trying to reach your full potential by getting better every single day."*

High performance is about the capacity to focus and concentrate.

There are distractions everywhere. So many things are vying for our attention. Gmail creator, Paul Buchheit, had this to say when it came to the importance of focus: *"I think focus is your most powerful weapon. At Google, we were all so focused on becoming the best in the world at what we do."*

Golf is a game that requires a special kind of focus. The best players in the world will tell you it's about mastering the ability to switch on and off. Rory McIlroy is a great example of someone who believes in the power of focus. Highly methodical in his training approach, Rory will usually choose one or two mental key areas to work on during practice or tournaments. Focus usually being one of those.

Learning to focus is a skill that needs to be consistently nurtured and practiced.

There are very few sports that require the focus and concentration of motorsports, especially Formula 1. With cars reaching up to 340 *km/h* and G-forces of up to 6G's when decelerating, Formula 1 drivers cannot afford to take their eyes and focus off the road for even a millisecond. A loss of concentration can be costly and sometimes even fatal.

With well over 20 seasons of racing Formula 1 cars behind him, Fernando Alonso is a two-time World Champion, and has driven for teams such as McLaren, Aston Martin, and Scuderia Ferrari. In an interview with the Spaniard whilst preparing for the 2024 season, Fernando said:

> *"I'm constantly thinking about ways of getting faster behind the wheel and being a better driver. In the off season, I will rewatch some of the races that happened the previous year as well and maybe you see different lines, different strategies for all the teams or drivers. So that curiosity from a driver point of view, of getting better, is always there and you never stop learning, and you never stop getting better. You have to be extremely focused. I call it 'Hyper Focus.' This is about having a total dedication to what you do. It's about paying*

attention to the small details. It's not letting any distractions get in the way of what you are trying to achieve."

Hyper focus is the ability to eliminate all distractions and be fully engaged in the present moment.

Staying on Formula 1, a few years back, I had a conversation with a team member at the Mercedes Benz Petronas Formula 1 team. It was someone who had worked closely with multiple World Champion, Lewis Hamilton. I asked her what characteristics of the British driver stood out. She mentioned that Lewis had many other interests besides racing a car, such as his love for music, fashion, and entertainment. Things that can so easily be a distraction.

But it was Lewis' ability to switch his focus from one thing to another and be completely present she was most impressed by. Even small things like media requests or fan engagement days, he would be able to switch his full attention from one thing to another. His focus and ability to be in the moment is incredible.

When you are focused, you pay attention to the smaller details better.

We know that frequent distractions affect our productivity. It takes longer to finish a task. We tend to not listen as well. We forget things, or can't recall information promptly, which affects our personal life and professional image.

That's why having focus, or *'hyperfocus'*, is so important to our performance. In this day and age, we are bombarded by a constant flow of information. Studies have shown that our brains are so primed for this distraction that just seeing our iPhone, for example, impairs our ability to concentrate.

> *What you focus on grows.*
> *What you think about expands.*
> *What you dwell upon determines your destiny.*

You might be asking at this stage, "Okay I get it, but how do I go about improving my focus?"

Improving your ability to focus can be done by performing a few simple exercises such as practicing mindfulness. Practicing mindfulness can be done by sitting in a chair, closing your eyes, and focusing on your breathing, for example. You could set an alarm for sixty seconds, and practice being fully present in that moment. Once you feel yourself improving, you can increase it from sixty seconds to seventy seconds and so on. It might take some time, and you'll probably have to remind yourself to keep at it, but with consistent practice, you'll begin to notice a difference in how well you can focus.

Improving your mental focus takes practice and patience.

A few years ago, I asked a Martial Arts Coach in Cincinnati, Ohio, what the key was to developing an elite level of focus and concentration. He said: *"Just like any other skill, learning how to properly focus takes many years to master. It requires thousands and thousands of repetitions. This builds muscle memory. The same thing occurs with our brains, how we retain information naturally is even more important when we are learning how to gain and maintain focus."*

The more your mind is present, the more focused you become.

One of the world's best cricketers was South Africa's, Jacque Kallis. Born in Cape Town, Kallis is the only cricketer (as of writing this) in the history of the game to score more than 10,000 runs and take over 250 wickets in both ODI and Test Match Cricket. When it came to focus, Kallis had a routine much like a golfer to maintain his concentration when batting. He would switch on, and then after the ball had been played, he would switch off again. In his words: *"It's impossible to concentrate for six and a half hours in the day, so I learned to focus for a few seconds at a time when required."*

When you learn to concentrate and focus, you improve your confidence. In pressure situations, you stay calmer and in control. This gives high performers the ability to calmly analyze situations and solve problems.

Focus gives high performers the mental edge.

Being able to focus and be in the moment is something the very best performers are able to do consistently. They have an ability to lock in and be totally absorbed in the present moment. They maintain this until they have completed their goal or mission.

Pete Carroll, the former NFL Super Bowl winning Coach of the Seattle Seahawks said this about the power of focus:

"It's the discipline of staying focused on what is right in front of you. It's the ability to not be distracted by what's going on, what just happened, or what's coming up. It takes tremendous discipline to do that, and it takes a massive commitment to find that consistency that keeps you from going in and out of focus.

It's about staying in the present and not getting too far ahead of yourself. At the elite level, you can't have inconsistency and a lack of focus."

Excellence is a product of deep focus.

I trust this chapter has highlighted that becoming great in a particular area requires a high level of focus and concentration. Don't let distractions derail you or get in the way of where you are heading. Stay focused, ignore the distractions, and you will accomplish your goals much faster.

F. Follow

O. One

C. Course

U. Until

S. Successful

CHAPTER 7

COACHABILITY

The most successful people I've encountered all have this one unique trait: COACHABILITY. They wake up each morning with a desire to learn something new. These people are lifelong learners.

In this chapter, we are going to answer the following key questions:

- What does it mean to be 'coachable'?

- What makes a coachable person?

- What qualities does a coachable person have that an uncoachable person doesn't?

- What benefits are there to being more coachable?

In a 2019 NCSA Recruiting Report, several College Coaches from a wide range of sports were asked to rank the following qualities in an athlete - character, athletic ability, academics, and location. The results? The majority of these College Coaches ranked character first, suggesting that they care more about an athlete's character than their skills and athleticism. Why is this? One of the reasons was that a person with the right character will be more coachable and open to learning new skills.

When it comes to recruiting or hiring, I like to use what I call the 3C's:

1. Character

2. Competence

3. Coachability

How coachable you are is closely linked to your character. Your character is linked to your personality and how you think and behave. The more coachable you are, the more competence you inherit.

Character is everything when it comes to hiring and recruiting. Get this wrong and it can cost you and your organization. In fact, **I would far prefer having someone in my team who is a 'B' in skill level, but an 'A' when it comes to their attitude. It's far easier to teach skills than it is to teach attitude.**

Let's be realistic, competence and skills matter. You need people who can do the job, but they don't have to be perfect. What matters most is their attitude and the energy they bring.

Skills matter. Let's face it,
you can't win the Kentucky Derby on a donkey!

Having the right character is one of the key principles of the New Zealand All Blacks Rugby team. Within their renowned "15 Principles," they make it clear that if you're not a good person, you won't play for them - no matter how good you are. They believe that *'Better people make better All Blacks.'*

Being coachable is a choice.

New York Times bestselling author Marshall Goldsmith recommends leaders within the corporate world should look for courage, humility and discipline when hiring. His belief is that courage determines the willingness of the person to try new things and step out of his or her comfort zone. Humility addresses a person's willingness to accept the fact that others count; *"It's not all about me."* And finally, discipline indicates whether a person has the drive to follow up and follow through so that change occurs.

A coachable person has the courage to change and the willingness to learn new things.

It's little surprise that the trait of being coachable is what the best leaders and job recruiters are looking for today. Just like in the 2019 NCSA Recruiting Report, it reaffirms that a student-athlete's coachability is as much a key part of the college recruiting process as athletic ability and academics.

It's also a known fact that coachable people adapt to change better. This is mainly because of their openness to learning new things. They embrace change and aren't stuck on autopilot. Coachable people are always willing to hear new ideas and test new theories.

Footballer Conor Bradley is a good example of a coachable athlete. Making his debut as a 19-year-old in Jurgen Klopp's Liverpool team in 2024, the Northern Ireland-born footballer was able to successfully hit the ground running in the team.

When a Coach from Conor's youth playing days was asked about his rise to the highest playing level, the one thing that stood out for him above all others, was that Conor was coachable. This former Coach said that when he would be chatting to the young players during practice, some would be messing about and not paying attention, but Conor would be completely focused, taking in every word. He listened with his eyes and ears.

"Conor was brilliant, always wanting to learn, and had a remarkable desire to improve and grow. He would ask me for some drills and exercises he could do at home. It's this focus

*and dedication that has taken him to where he
is today."*

**Coachable people don't only listen with their ears,
but their eyes. They observe every word being spoken.**

One afternoon during a practice session with Rafael Nadal in Madrid, I was chatting with his Coach, Carlos Moya. I asked Carlos what it was like coaching 'Rafa,' to which he replied: *"I think I would find it difficult to work with any other player because Rafa is just so coachable and just wants to keep improving. He is curious and asks a lot of questions. Even after winning all those Grand Slam titles, he just wants to keep getting better."*

**High performers never get complacent.
No matter how good they become,
they are always looking for ways to get better.**

If you're coachable you have a different relationship with feedback and criticism. You don't take it personally or feel like a victim. You have the humility and curiosity to listen. You have the maturity to understand that feedback and criticism are there to help you improve and grow.

The Three Doors to Learning and Growth:

1. Humility
2. Curiosity
3. Open-mindedness

I remember asking a CEO at a Leader's Conference in Seattle a few years ago about what she looked for when it came to finding the right people for her organization. She said: *"You need to find people with good values and the right attitude. You also need to find people who already possess the skills and abilities to perform at a high level. But the most important one is coachability. If they aren't willing to learn and grow, you won't make progress."*

> *A closed-minded and uncoachable person will eventually become a liability for your team or organization.*

On being asked what it was like to coach Lebron James, Cleveland Cavaliers Assistant Coach, Phil Handy said: *"LeBron James is the ultimate professional and is a dream to work with because, despite being the best player in the game, he remains very coachable. You would expect guys like that to be hard [to coach], but he knows the game, is a student of the game, studies,* wants to be challenged, and he wants to be coached. Every day he strives to be better than the day before."

Upbringing influences coachability. It all starts in the home.

I personally believe that coachability starts in the home. We are all influenced by our upbringing and home life. Family values and ethics play a major part in this process. The most coachable athletes and people I have worked with all came from families where good values, respect, and discipline were ingrained.

If there would be just one piece of advice I could share with all the parents out there, it would be to teach your child how to be coachable. This is possible by reminding your kids that criticism and feedback are necessary to learn, grow and improve.

Being coachable is very much about having respect.

When it comes to being coachable, Cristiano Ronaldo, seen as one of the best Football players in history, said: *"When I was 18, playing at Manchester United, some of the more senior players in the team would give me advice, and I took that as help to improve, because they knew more than me. This new generation, I feel, most don't accept criticism. If you don't want my help and my advice, then how can you improve? Look at yourself, do your best to help the team."*

Regardless of upbringing, coachability is still a choice. It's never too late to want to learn and grow.

5 Traits of a Coachable Person:

1. **They are Open to Feedback** – They are willing to receive feedback and adapt it to make improvements. They welcome new ideas and thoughts.

2. **They Stay Accountable** – A coachable person takes responsibility for their actions and choices.

3. **They are Deeply Curious** – A coachable person is always curious about what they don't know. They aren't 'know it all' people. They are always seeking new ways to do things better.

4. **They are Active Listeners** – Active listening involves paying attention to what the other person is saying. A coachable person listens with all their senses. They look the other person in the eyes and absorb everything they are saying.

5. **They Love to Ask Questions** – A coachable person asks questions. They want to find out as much as possible, and they do this by being proactive and asking questions.

A coachable person doesn't just wait for feedback, they ask for it.

A coachable person doesn't just wait for feedback, they ask for it. Steve Kerr, Head Coach of the Golden State Warriors Basketball team said that Steph Curry, their standout player, was one such player who proactively asked for feedback on how he could get better.

After practice, Steph would ask Coach Kerr and his coaching staff questions like: *"What did I do well today?" "What do I need to work on most?"* and *"How can I improve this?"* Steph would then immediately grab one of the trainers to help him work on what he'd been advised.

Asking for feedback speeds up the learning process.

I recently listened to a podcast with Brian Chesky, the Co-Founder and CEO of Airbnb, as a guest. Chesky was talking about the importance of communication and feedback within his organization. He said: *"Shameless people learn really quickly and are successful. Most people are just afraid to ask people for feedback or help. We are shameless here about asking people for feedback, whether it's our investors, or meeting famous entrepreneurs like Mark Zuckerberg or Jeff Bezos or Warren Buffett. You know, the best way is to seek out people and ask them for feedback. Most people are really nice, and they'll help you if they can."*

Having worked closely with athletes for over 25 years, I was quickly able to tell who was coachable and who wasn't. How was I able to do this you ask? Through observing where their attention was when a coach or someone was speaking. I would notice their body language and the way they would engage. A coachable person looks interested in what the other person is saying, absorbing every word being spoken.

*"My best skill was that I was coachable.
I was a sponge and aggressive to learn."*

– Michael Jordan

Most noticeably, the coachable players would be the ones to arrive at practice early and want to be pushed by their coach. I learned that the time at which a person arrives for practice tells you a lot about their commitment for improvement.

The coachable ones are proactive when it comes to their learning and growth. They are also willing to experience discomfort in order to evolve and grow and improve.

Some will argue that everyone is coachable. I tend to disagree, as I have often come across athletes who might not like or connect with a coach. This can result in them shutting down and disengaging.

The late Rita Pierson, a teacher from Texas, gave one of the most watched TED talks ever. She said: *"Kids don't learn from people they don't like."* It's a powerful comment because it displays how our relationship with another person can directly affect our coachability. However, I believe that a coachable person is able to separate the message from the person. This takes an element of maturity. Being mature enough to realize that we can learn from anyone, even if we don't like them, is an enviable characteristic.

A coachable person is open to learning from anyone.

A coachable person understands that feedback and constructive criticism is meant to help them improve and not to be taken personally. They want to hear the truth. Famed longtime NBA Coach, Doc Rivers once said: *"Average players want to be left alone. Good players want to be coached. Great players want to be told the truth."*

A coachable person is invested in their own progress and development.

How can you tell if someone is uncoachable?

- An uncoachable person feels like they are being 'called out' when they receive feedback

- An uncoachable person believes they already have all the answers

- An uncoachable person will judge others and those who are sharing the feedback

- An uncoachable person wants to be in control and tell others how things should be done

- An uncoachable person, when receiving feedback, will usually start with a negative reaction or display a closed-off body language.

During the March Madness Tournament in 2024, Caitlin Clark, regarded as one of the greatest players in College Basketball history, said: *"I never want to stop being told what's right, or what's wrong. No matter how good I play or how bad I play. There are always things to learn, things to get better at. She* [her coach] *holds me to a very high standard and yeah, she's going to get on me because she knows there's still areas for me to improve on. She holds me to a high standard in that regard, and that's something I really appreciate about her."*

*A coachable person is okay with admitting
"I don't know the answer to that,
but I'm willing to find it out."*

To be coachable, a person must be willing to be vulnerable at times. Not everyone feels comfortable admitting they have weaknesses or limiting factors. However, when you are willing to admit these things, and open yourself up to learning and improving, that's when the real progress begins. A coachable person will ask for help when they need it.

Seeing vulnerability as a weakness, rather than strength and courage, prohibits us from being really authentic. You can't grow if you can't be authentic with yourself and others. Best-selling Author Brene Brown said: *"Vulnerability is not weakness. And that myth is profoundly dangerous."*

*True humility is staying teachable,
regardless of how much you think you already know.*

During a trip to Brisbane, Australia one year, I had a conversation with a well-known Australian Rules Football (or "Aussie Rules") coach. I asked how he was able to make quick decisions during a game when it came to making replacements, etc. He said: *"Allistair, it's pretty simple to be honest. The players I trust to put on the field in clutch situations are the men that have set their egos aside and have confidence in themselves and their teammates to perform at a high level. These players are always coachable and open to learning as much as possible. They have faith in me as a coach, which in turn, gives me the faith in them to go out and perform. Simply put, the players that are coachable are the players that I trust to put in tough situations."*

No greatness happens without having the humility to listen and be coached.

Last but not least, something I strongly believe is that if you are the same person you were a year ago, or even six months ago, you haven't embraced growth and learning enough. One thing I always like to remind myself is that if I don't look back a year ago and cringe at some of the things I said or did, I haven't learned enough. That's why I believe it's so important to stay coachable and keep learning. If you aren't learning, you aren't growing.

So let me ask you, *"How coachable are you?"*

Your level of growth comes down to how coachable and open you are to learning new things.

– Allistair McCaw

CHAPTER 8

EFFORT

Success is never an accident. It's a result of a commitment to excellence and a relentless work ethic.

Former Coach of the Miami Heat Basketball team Pat Riley once said: *"If you have a positive attitude and constantly strive to give your best effort, eventually you will overcome your immediate problems and find you are ready for greater challenges."*

No one succeeds without putting in the effort and time. Robert Collier, a renowned self-help author, said: *"Success is the sum of small efforts, repeated day in and day out."* I love this quote as it highlights the enduring nature of excellence, emphasizing that it is not a result of one grand gesture, but rather the accumulation of consistent daily efforts.

Collier's quote encourages and reminds us to focus on the small actions we take each day, as they contribute to long-term success. He reminds us that greatness doesn't happen in a day; it doesn't happen in a week, or a month, or even a year.

Greatness takes years of consistent effort.

By consistently working towards your goals, no matter how small the steps may seem, you can ultimately achieve remarkable outcomes over time. That's why persistence and patience are the cornerstones to achieving something worthwhile.

Keep making the steps, no matter how big or small.
Each step edges you closer to your goal.

There is a great video on YouTube of College Basketball Coach, Geno Auriemma. In this video, he is speaking to his players at a practice session touching on the following points:

- Great players not only possess the skills, but they also work hard and make an effort in every aspect of the game, especially in training

- Great players give 100% in every play and drills, regardless of whether they are the star players or not

- Effort is a crucial factor in achieving success and building a winning team culture

- Energy level and effort is something that every great player brings to the court

What Coach Auriemma talks about doesn't only apply to athletes or sports; it applies to life - especially when it comes to achieving your best. My favorite line in this video is when he says: *"We're not here to coach your effort and energy level. That's a given".*

Attitude and effort are on you.
No one should have to ask that of you.

If there is something I've learned from watching the best performers in their fields, it's this: They are not afraid of failure and they keep putting in maximum effort. They don't let a mistake or setback interfere with their performance and greater goals.

The best performers all hold effort as a standard.

One of the differences between the best performers and those a level below is the consistent attitude and effort they give daily. The best performers still give their best effort especially on the days when they aren't feeling their best or things aren't going to plan. They don't allow their emotions to dictate their level of output.

A Champion gives their best effort,
regardless of how they feel.

The truth is, you can't be at your best every time you step out to perform. It's impossible. Not even the best performers in the world achieve this. The best performers understand they can't control outcomes or results. They also know that their best effort doesn't always guarantee the outcome they desire. What they most understand is if they don't give their best effort, their chances of succeeding are minimal.

The key factor is in **how** you show up on the days when you aren't feeling it, or when things aren't going to plan. How you deal with these factors ultimately determines how mentally tough you are. Let's face it, everyone is good on their good days but how good are you on the lesser days? That's the real question you should be asking yourself.

Effort requires no special talent, only a choice.

No matter how you feel, always show up. Put in the work each and every day. When you stack these hard-working days on top of each other, you will eventually reap the rewards. Winston Churchill said: *"Continuous effort, not strength or intelligence, is the key to unlocking our potential."*

Winners keep putting in the effort no matter what. This is how they develop grit and a growth mindset.

They understand this improves their abilities and intelligence. People with a growth mindset are more likely to embrace challenges, seek feedback, learn from mistakes, and persist in the face of adversities. Grit is a result of effort.

Effort is about what you are willing to give.

I've always believed that being true to yourself is a powerful characteristic. Only we know when we are lying to ourselves. Only we know if we gave our best effort or not. As a child, I remember teachers and coaches would ask me: *"Allistair, did you give your best effort?"* That question would always sink deep into the pit of my stomach. I knew it was a question that I had to answer honestly to myself.

For parents, when it comes to sports and school, the best questions to ask your kids are not: *"Did you get an A?"* or *"Did you win?"* Instead, ask them: *"Did you honestly give your best effort?"* and *"Do you really believe you tried your hardest?"* Aim to focus on the things they **CAN** control.

Focus on rewarding the controllables.

When we place value in the effort, we celebrate the process. When we value the effort, we are showing that when you give your best, it's good enough. This approach boosts self-esteem and confidence because individuals recognize their worth is not based on a specific result or outcome, but on their dedication and application to hard work. Here's the thing about effort: Even though people don't always notice when you try hard, they will certainly notice when you don't.

Aim for a perfect effort, not a perfect outcome.

It requires no special talent to put in your best effort. Showing up and working hard is one of the most important traits and habits needed to achieve successful outcomes. Ignore the opportunity to cut corners or take shortcuts. When you take shortcuts, it becomes a poor habit that eventually ends up costing you more in the long run.

While many people think talent is crucial, it's attitude, work ethic, and effort that propels an individual from good to great. Many have regretted the wrong preparation or strategy, but no one has ever regretted putting in the right effort. Former Denver Broncos Quarterback, Peyton Manning said: *"During my 18 year career in the NFL, I might at times have left the field wondering if a different strategy or tactics could have worked better. But one thing I never questioned myself on was my level of effort."*

Effort is controllable. No one else can control how much effort you are willing to put in. Only you can decide that. 99% of the time we have no control of the outcome as there are a million other factors that come into play. We do, however, control 100% of our effort level. No one else can influence that. You control your effort completely - don't ever forget that.

One of the most powerful pieces ever written was from Theodore Roosevelt called, *"The Man in the Arena."* It goes:

> *"It is not the critic who counts, not the man who points out how the strong man stumbles, or where the doer of deeds could have done better. The credit belongs to the man who is actually in the arena, whose face is marred by dust and sweat and blood, who strives valiantly, who errs and comes up short again and again, because there is no effort without error or shortcoming, but who knows the great enthusiasms, the great devotions, who spends himself for a worthy cause; who, at the best, knows in the end the triumph of high achievement, and who, at the worst, if he fails, at least he fails while daring greatly, so that his place shall never be with those cold and timid souls who knew neither victory nor defeat."*

What I love about this piece from Roosevelt is that it places the importance and value on effort and the character of a person. Effort is about the courage to fail and keep trying until you succeed. Your success will be measured by your willingness to keep on trying.

A winner's mindset is all about the effort.
The right effort leads to excellence.
The wrong effort leads to disappointment and regret.

In life, we get what we give. You can't expect to be a winner if you don't put in a winning effort. Michael Jordan once said: *"Be true to the game, because the game will be true to you. If you try to shortcut the game, then the game will shortcut you. If you put forth the effort, good things will be bestowed upon you. That's truly about the game, and in some ways that's about life too."*

Making it to the top requires giving
a maximum effort.

There is a reason why the best are the best. It's not that they have more talent than the others. It's because they are willing to stay disciplined and consistent in giving their best effort. They understand that effort is more important than talent because over time, effort leads to better skill ability.

The great Track Runner Jesse Ownes once said: *"We all have dreams. But in order to make dreams into reality, it takes an awful lot of determination, dedication, self-discipline, and effort."*

One of the World's best Footballers, Cristiano Ronaldo said: *"Talent without work is nothing. Work without talent is nothing. Everyone wants to be Cristiano. Even if I give you the map, it's difficult. It's all about discipline. The work. The effort. Not only in sport, but in life. The main point is this: Are you willing to do that?"*

The results you get will usually be in direct proportion to your preparation and the effort you give. Let me ask you this: How hard are you willing to work? How much effort are you willing to give? How much extra work are you willing to put in? – These things will massively influence your future success.

No one became great by doing just 'enough.'

Enough might make you good, but it's not enough to become great. No one got to the top by cruising along. They put in the extra time and effort others weren't willing to do. They committed themselves to always giving their best.

Talking about how much effort you give is cheap. Effort isn't found in your words. Effort is found in your behaviors and the actions you take. These will ultimately prove how much effort you are willing to give.

I encourage you to bring your best no matter your goals. Don't spend your time worrying about outcomes. Focus on the controllables like giving a 100% effort and then trust that the outcome will be exactly as it is meant to be.

Remember that in life, what you put in is what you will get out. Your effort will always be rewarded. This may not occur straight away. Mark W. Boyer said: *"The effort you put forth in whatever you do is directly proportional to the results you produce."*

The amount of effort you give is up to you. Trust me, there is no better feeling than going to bed at the end of each day and being able to say: *"Today I gave my best and I'm proud of that. Tomorrow I will do the same."* This is the mindset of a Champion.

You don't need to tell others how invested you are. Your level of effort will show that.

– Allistair McCaw

CHAPTER 9

EMPOWERING SELF-TALK

erhaps you haven't realized it, but we are constantly in conversation with ourselves. The most successful people I've come across talk to themselves like winners. They understand the biggest influence to their success is the voice inside their head.

They say that only crazy people talk to themselves but isn't it usually these people who go on to achieve great things? Staying average doesn't create excellence. Staying average instead creates, well, average.

How you talk to yourself is everything. The words you say can be the difference between success and failure. Your self-talk and inner voice have the power to steer you in any direction you choose. Words are powerful.

Your words hold the power to steer you in any direction.

You can pretty much talk yourself into, or out of, almost anything. With a strong mindset and empowering self-talk, you can achieve more than you could ever imagine.

It's no surprise that empowering and positive self-talk improves your self-esteem, confidence, and wellbeing.

> *"A strong, positive self-image is the best possible preparation for success."*
>
> – Joyce Brothers

Your words hold power. What you tell yourself repeatedly will eventually become your beliefs. If you think like a winner, you will become a winner. The opposite is true as well. If you repeatedly tell yourself that you can't do something, the chances are, that is what will happen.

When watching a sports event, you will sometimes see athletes talking to themselves. What they are doing is affirming their beliefs and strengths. These are positive mantras and self-affirmations athletes are injecting their minds and body.

Arguably the greatest Gymnast of all time, Simone Biles, could often be seen mouthing words of encouragement to herself before competing. In the 2024 Paris Olympics, just before starting her floor routine, Simone said to herself: *"You've got this!"*

Positive self-talk can improve your performance.

It doesn't matter what the situation or event is. It could be getting up to speak in front of a large audience or standing on the start line of a race - the words you say to yourself can fuel your confidence and propel you to your best performance. In fact, before I go up on stage to speak, I always give myself a little encouraging pep talk.

By actively working on improving your self-talk, you directly enhance both your personal and professional performances. This helps build your confidence. When it comes to speaking and presenting in front of people, it certainly has helped mine!

Building confidence comes from the way you talk to yourself.

To take better control of your performances, you need to take control of your thoughts, emotions, and attention. The more control you have of your mind, the better you'll perform.

We all get negative thoughts; it's part of being human. However, the difference between a positive and negative person is that a positive person will still get negative thoughts, but they are able to let go of them quicker. They don't let a negative thought hang around.

Positive people don't let negative thoughts hang around.

Golfing great, Tiger Woods, was once asked what the difference was between the world's best golfers and the rest. His answer? – *"The best in the world are able to let go of their last mistake quicker. They can move on and not let it affect them"*. How do they do this? By focusing on the next play and saying something positive to themselves.

Winners have a strong inner belief they will succeed. Is this arrogance? Not at all. Arrogance can be described as feeling the need to be loud and vocal about it. True confidence, on the other hand, is when you have an inner stillness and don't feel the need to advertise it. True confidence is about having a healthy relationship with yourself.

Believe in your ability to succeed.

Success all starts in the mind. The thoughts and words you say to yourself have the greatest influence on this. Winners talk to themselves like winners. Their thoughts become their actions and behaviors. Their actions and behaviors become their outcomes.

After winning his second major title at The Open in 2024, professional Golfer Xander Schauffele, said: *"I believe in positive self-talk. I talk to myself all the time. When you believe something enough, it will happen."*

Greatness cannot happen without a mindset that fuels you, pushes you, and empowers you. An empowering mindset is one that reminds you that you have what it takes, no matter the odds. An empowering mindset instills faith and belief in yourself.

Benefits of Empowering Self-Talk:

- Improved performance
- Increased confidence and self-esteem
- More joy in what you are doing
- Better outcomes and results
- Better ability to cope with emotions and stress
- Increased optimism and resilience
- Increased motivation
- Less performance anxiety

Your greatest opponent isn't somebody else. It's you. It's the voice inside your head.

An empowering mindset will help you to keep looking forwards and channel your energy into finding solutions, especially when adversity arrives and things get challenging. We can't choose what thoughts come into our heads, but we can choose how long we allow those thoughts to stay there.

In sports, I've seen many athletes self-sabotage their own performances time and time again through doubt and negative self-talk. They might have prepared well, but then find every reason under the sun as to why they can't do something. In the end, they defeat themselves.

How does one overcome this kind of defeatist mindset? The answer is by both recognizing it and then going to work on it. Having an awareness of what your thoughts are is key.

When you can control the mind, you win.

Like anything else, your self-talk and mindset are a skill that needs to be practiced. Just like learning to play a sport or musical instrument, you need to intentionally work on these skills daily if you want to become good at it.

The mind is no different. The world's best performers intentionally work on their mindset and awareness skills daily. This includes their self-talk and control of thoughts. By doing this, they are better equipped to catch themselves in the act when a negative thought pops up in their head.

Your words matter. Negative self-talk can have a detrimental effect on a person's self-image, self-esteem, and belief in their self-worth and abilities. Nothing weighs heavier than negativity. When you realize just how much the words you say to yourself influences your happiness, outcomes, and life in general, you become more cognizant of what you say to yourself.

Nothing weighs more than negativity.

Why do we berate ourselves over a mistake or failure? It's because we haven't established stopguards, boundaries, or standards for ourselves. That's why having a rule that you're only allowed to use words that empower you should be put in place. Just think about it for a second... Would you say some of the things you say to yourself to someone you love or your best friend? Probably not. Then why say them to yourself?

Research has shown that we are far better at encouraging or advising other people than ourselves. I can relate to this fully.

Make sure your worst enemy is not living between your ears.

Having good self-awareness is key. Catching yourself in the act when saying something negative, and immediately replacing it with something positive, is a learned and practiced skill. The more you practice, the better your self-talk will become. This is where true transformation occurs.

The way you talk to yourself creates your reality.

Try to pay attention to the words you say to yourself (especially after making a mistake). If it's not positive and helpful, then immediately replace it with a positive thought. Over time, this is how you build a more empowering mindset.

Like anything else, your self-talk is a skill that needs daily practice. It doesn't require a special talent. When you believe in the skills you have, and your ability to succeed, you can propel yourself towards success.

Developing empowering self-talk requires no special talent, just practice.

When you stop doubting yourself, your belief and confidence rises. You talk to yourself in a more uplifting way. When you think more positively about yourself, you feel a different energy and motivation. Self-empowerment through self-talk is a skill we should practice every day. It's a skill we learn and then choose to use. It will become more natural the more we practice it.

When you upgrade your mindset,
you upgrade your life.

3 Ways to Become a More Positive Thinker:

1. **Recognize it!**

   Aim to be more aware of the thoughts and words you're saying to yourself. Just the act of recognizing negative thoughts for what they are, is the first step to working through the problem.

2. **Replace it!**

   When a negative thought arises, immediately stop the thought in its track and replace it with something more positive and helpful.

3. **Reward it!**

   The best way to improve in something is to compliment yourself when you perform the first two steps above. Even by saying something simple to yourself like, *"Way to go me!"* will encourage you as you go about changing your thinking for the better.

Watch what you say to yourself.
You're likely to believe it.

I've never met a person with a negative mindset who lives a positive life. It doesn't exist. The control of your thoughts and your self-talk play the biggest role in this. Incorporating positive self-talk can have a profound impact on your mindset and overall well-being. Learn to replace negative self-talk with affirmations that uplift and empower you. Over time, you will notice a positive shift in your mindset, increased self-confidence, and a greater sense of joy and fulfillment in your life.

Shifting our self-talk and using language that increases our energy leads to a more fulfilling life.

As I mentioned earlier in this chapter, self-affirmations are a great way to develop your self-talk. Affirmations are powerful statements that can help shift your mindset from a negative space to a positive one. Saying encouraging words to yourself, such as *"I've got this!"* or *"I love taking on a difficult challenge!"* will empower and motivate you.

By using affirmations and mantras you can replace negative beliefs with positive ones.

Below are 10 self-affirmation examples to help you improve your self-talk and self-esteem:

1. *"I am ready"*
2. *"I can do this"*
3. *"I am confident"*
4. *"I am worthy"*
5. *"I am unstoppable"*
6. *"I am strong"*
7. *"I am growing each day"*
8. *"I am ready to compete like a Champion"*
9. *"I can do anything I put my mind to"*
10. *"Today is going to be a great day"*

Self-talk is the most powerful form of communication. It can either empower you or defeat you.

– Allistair McCaw

CHAPTER 10

GRIT

nyone who has achieved success will tell you that it involved overcoming numerous obstacles and challenges. Nothing worth achieving ever comes easy. In fact, I am yet to come across a successful person who hasn't gone through their fair share of trials and difficulties.

Actor Chuck Norris once said*: "I've always found that anything worth achieving will always have obstacles in the way, and you've got to have that drive and determination to overcome those obstacles on route to whatever it is that you want to accomplish."*

There's no shine without the grind.

In this chapter, we are going to cover three specific areas that are vital to maximizing your potential and achieving greatness.

1. Developing Grit
2. Learning from Failure
3. Managing Adversity and Pressure

1. Developing Grit

What is grit? According to Angela Duckworth, a Psychologist and Researcher famous for bringing attention to the term 'grit', describes it as having a passion and perseverance for long term and meaningful goals. In her words: *"Grit is the ability to endure hardship."*

Grit is the stubborn refusal to quit.

When you have grit, you are able to push through the more difficult tasks. Grit is what Champions have built over many years. Grit is the stubborn refusal to quit. Dustin Poirier, the UFC Champion Fighter said: *"Grit, determination, the right amount of crazy, self-belief - everything it takes to be a Champion. I have that."*

Interestingly, in life, the strongest people are usually those who have overcome the most. They have taken life by the horns. They have an archive of difficult experiences that have made them who they are today.

Grit is about bouncing back after a setback.

Michael Jordan is widely regarded as the greatest Basketball player of all time but what many don't know is that he initially didn't even make his high school Basketball team. As a fifteen-year-old hoping to make it onto the squad, Michael tried out along with about 50 of his classmates, but there were only 15 spots available. At the time, Michael was only 5'10" and couldn't yet dunk a basketball, which resulted in not being selected, much to his devastation.

MJ didn't, however, let the rejection stop him. He turned this painful experience into motivation. It gave Michael the determination and willpower to become one of the greatest athletes of all time.

"You have a choice!
You can throw in the towel, or you can use it
to wipe the sweat off your face!"

– Anonymous

Michael's story is a lesson for all of us because if you quit when things get tough, it gets that much easier to quit the next time. Problematically, this can then become a habit. However, if you force yourself to push through it and endure, you begin to develop the grit needed for you to grow.

The more struggle you endure, the more grit you gain.

Grit is about building daily habits that allow you to stick to a schedule and overcome challenges. **To be mentally tough, you don't have to be more skilled,**

talented or intelligent – just more disciplined and consistent. Many believe that mental toughness is all about working hard and pushing your own limits, when in fact, it's more about discipline and consistency.

With every difficult experience and obstacle you are able to overcome, you build more grit. That's why some of the most successful people in the world have overcome many failures and disappointments, and gone on to achieve great things.

NBA Basketball player, Aaron Gordon said: *"Developing a resiliency, a grit, a level of poise, a composure, a level of perspective, confidence, courage, compassion are all things you can work on daily."*

> *Building grit is like training a muscle in the body. The more you train it, the stronger it gets.*

A few years ago, I set myself the challenge of running seven full marathons, seven half-marathons, seven 10Ks, and seven 5Ks in seven weeks. I prepared for this challenge for a full year, carefully planning and monitoring my progress, and in doing this, I set three goals for this challenge.

The first goal was, of course, to complete all 7 weeks. The second goal was to experiment on recovery techniques to see what worked or didn't. Ice baths, hot baths, cryotherapy, recovery gels, you name it, I was prepared for it. My third and final goal was to see how I would mentally cope.

It was only after the third week that my body started to rebel and fight me. In doing so, my mind began to whisper that maybe this challenge I'd set myself was a bit too ambitious. It was during the 4th week running a marathon in Montreal, I hit the proverbial wall (runners will know this term well). At about the 37-kilometer mark, my body didn't want to cooperate. That's when I tapped into the mental side of things.

I had two mantras I would say to myself. The first was: *"Every step is one step closer to my goal - keep going!"* And the second mantra was: *"I didn't come this far to only get this far."* These two mantras are what eventually gave me the extra motivation to complete my goal of seven full marathons, seven half-marathons, seven 10Ks, and seven 5Ks in seven weeks!

Grit is about pushing through the difficult challenges.

Interestingly, my fastest marathon of those seven weeks came at the final one in West Palm Beach, Florida where I ran 3 hours and 9 minutes. It was a sweltering 36 degrees celsius that day, and more than half of the runners didn't finish the race. Through grit and determination, I had trained my mind to be the strongest muscle in my body. Even though I couldn't stop unhelpful thoughts from entering my mind, I did have the power to control how long I allowed them to stay there. The lesson from this experiment was: Developing the right mindset, not accepting excuses, and committing to your goals, builds grit and resilience.

Grit is the reward you get when you overcome difficulties.

2. Learning from Failure

I've learned, over time, that many people don't live up to their true potential, not because they lack the abilities or skills, but because they fear failure. The fear of failure can cripple some people. Their thoughts and self-talk become filled with doubt. Their fear is channeled towards unhelpful thoughts, like what others will think of them if they fail.

Nothing is scarier than avoiding your full potential.

Ever since I was a young boy, I've been a risk taker. Some risks have paid off and some have failed miserably. I have a belief that later in life it is our inactions to take risks that we wish we could undo the most. In her best-selling book, *"Top 5 Regrets of the Dying,"* Bronnie Ware writes that the number one regret of the dying was that they wished they had had the courage to live a life true to themselves, not the life others expected of them.

When people realize that their life is almost over, and begin to reflect, it is easy to see how many goals and dreams have gone unfulfilled. Most people had not honored even half of their dreams and had to die knowing that it was due to choices they had made, or not made. Isn't that sad?

Don't die with the music still in you.

I've discovered that those who have gone on to achieve greatness had a completely different relationship with risk and failure. They learned that in order to succeed, you have to embrace failing. They understand that failure is a part of success, not the opposite of it.

Greatness is closely linked to failure.

Multiple Formula One World Champion, Lewis Hamilton understands how closely linked greatness and failure are. In his words: *"Failure is 100% necessary for greatness. To achieve greatness and have success, you've got to fail as many times as possible. So don't shy away from it or take it as a negative. Every single successful person who has achieved great things, whether climbing Mount Everest or getting to the top of a company - they've all failed more times than they'll be able to remember. That's how they become great. No one has been great from the beginning. Failure is 100% necessary for greatness."*

Success never comes without a price. That price usually comes in the form of difficult challenges and setbacks. Unfortunately, many people quit due to having unrealistic expectations of what it takes to succeed. Remember, that success was never meant to be easy.

EXPECTATION

REALITY

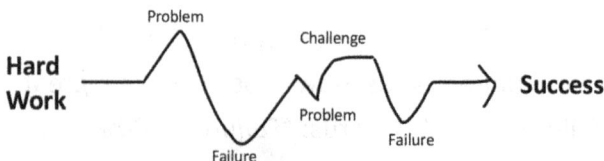

High performers believe the more they fail, the closer they get to success. Their failures became their most valuable lessons. These lessons have developed life skills and grit. If you asked them how they achieved this, they would most likely tell you that the first step to overcoming adversity is expecting and accepting it. Once you come to terms with the reality in front of you, you can start to embrace it and work towards making things better.

Thomas Edison famously once said in response to being asked how it felt to fail that many times while trying to invent the lightbulb: *"I didn't fail 1,000 times. The lightbulb was an invention with 1,000 steps."* Edison's attitude towards failure was part of the reason that made him successful.

High performers view setbacks and failure as a pathway to success, not an obstacle.

Even though nobody sets out to fail, failure gives us a chance to recover, reset, and learn from our mistakes. Each experience, whether good or bad, teaches us something. It gives us an opportunity to learn, adjust, and grow.

Many a Champion and high performer has had adversity or failed at some stage of their life, but like Zig

Ziglar said: *"It's not how far you fall, but how high you bounce that counts."*

One of the greatest leaders of our time, former South African President, Nelson Mandela once said: *"Do not judge me by my successes, judge me by how many times I fell down and got back up again."* I love this quote from the great man as I often like to measure the success of someone not by what they have achieved, but what they had to overcome in order to achieve it.

People who are more growth-minded believe that intelligence and skills can be developed and grown through practice and effort. They view failures or setbacks as opportunities for growth and advancing their skill sets.

In the early days of Amazon, Jeff Bezos failed over and over, but he would use his failures as good reminders to keep improving in all areas. Failures for the now multi-billionaire were viewed as a learning experience and pathway to the next big discovery.

Failure is not the opposite of success - it's a part of it.

Growth-minded people generally aren't afraid to fail. They take more risks. They constantly like to challenge and stretch themselves. People with a more fixed mindset don't deal well with failure and avoid the process of struggle. They don't like to look bad in front of others. They fail to learn that our failures teach us more than our successes. The sooner we understand that failure is our friend and is there to teach us, we make progress. The most important thing is to understand why you failed.

After a failure or setback, ask yourself:

- Why did this happen?
- What have I learned from this?
- What would I do differently next time?
- How can this make me better?

When you are able to view adversity, failure, and setbacks as learning opportunities - you learn and grow. These failures and experiences are the key to success. Each one teaches us something.

The greatest failure is never trying at all. That only leaves regret. Michael Jordan once said: *"I can accept failure, everyone fails at something. But I can't accept not trying."*

Every part of failure eventually makes us successful.

In a 2024 commencement speech at Dartmouth College, former World number one Tennis player Roger

Federer said: *"You need to become a master at overcoming the harder moments. That, to me, is the sign of a Champion. The best in the world are not the best because they win every point. It's because they know they'll lose again and again, but they've learned how to deal with it."*

The best don't avoid or try to forget their mistakes but they don't dwell on them either. They embrace them, learn from them, and move on. When asked what made him such a great player, Federer simply replied: *"I tend to let go of the last mistake quicker."*

Obstacles and challenges are there to help us develop grit, resilience, and wisdom.

The best of the best fail forwards. In other words, they don't see failures as a setback, only a set up. From these adversities, they grow and make progress. They use them as the steppingstones to build grit and resilience.

Simone Biles is a great example of this having withdrawn from the 2020 Tokyo Olympics due to mental health reasons. The unstoppable American bounced back at the Paris 2024 Olympics to claim gold in the All-Around Final - a display of courage and resilience.

Those who tend to bounce back from failure quicker have a growth mindset.

Troy Bennett said: *"The one who falls and gets up is stronger than the one who never tried. Do not fear failure but rather fear not trying."*

Similarly, Denis Waitley once said: *"Failure should be our teacher, not our undertaker. Failure is delay, not defeat. It is a temporary detour, not a dead end. Failure is something we can avoid only by saying nothing, doing nothing, and being nothing."*

3. Managing Adversity and Pressure

Growing up, Simone Biles made many sacrifices to become the best. Her parents were unable to care for her; her mother struggled with addiction. She remembers her life before foster care, and having to eat cereal with water because the family could not afford milk.

She was soon adopted into a family where she was taught to be confident and proud. A multiple Olympic Champion, Simone excelled in her sport, representing the USA, and has inspired many people not only because of her accomplishments, but also because of her courage and ability to overcome adversity.

Actor and comedian, Jim Carrey, grew up in a family that struggled financially, and he often had to work odd jobs to help support them. He discovered his talent for comedy at a young age and began performing at local comedy clubs. Carrey's big break came in the early

1990s when he was cast in the hit sketch comedy show, *'In Living Color'*. He has gone on to earn a reputation as one of Hollywood's top comedic talents.

So, what was it that made both Simone Biles and Jim Carrey successful in their fields? It was perseverance and a dogged determination to become the best at what they do. Through the hardships, they both developed grit and resilience and neither played the victim card or 'woe-is-me' mentality.

Winners have a victor mentality.

Amy Morin, best-selling Author of the book, *"13 Things Mentally Strong People Do"*, said: *"Being a top performer - whether it's in business or on the athletic field - requires grit and tenacity, as well as the continuous desire to become better."*

Of course, there are many forms of adversity. Dealing with a death of a relative or battling a life-threatening illness are extreme adversities compared to an athlete missing a penalty kick in a Football game, for example. Difficult things can challenge us. We may fail several times. It may feel like a huge struggle. You may feel like giving up but something in you keeps on going. You keep pushing. You stick with it. This is grit.

When it comes to the pressure moments in sports, you will usually discover that it's the great athletes who are able to step up and perform. The main reason why is because of the mindset they have adopted and their preparation.

Croatian Footballer and Real Madrid star Luka Modric is one such example. When Luka was playing for the under-21 National team, his coach at the time Slavan Billic said: *"Luka is a leader on the field, not by shouting, but by taking responsibility. He always wants the ball when the pressure is on. Luka is a player who thrives under pressure."*

Pressure can be defined as *a 'form of stress that occurs because of how events in one's external or internal environment are perceived, resulting in the psychological experience of distress and anxiety' (Lazarus & Folkman, 1984).* In other words, it's our minds and how we perceive stress and pressure that strongly influence and determine how we manage and view it.

The world's top performers deal with pressure best due to the way they <u>view</u> it, <u>prepare</u> for it and <u>deal</u> with it.

In my book, *Habits That Make a Champion,* I explain the key reason why the World's top performers are where they are. It's due to how they view pressure, prepare for it, and deal with it. How you view pressure is everything. You can either see it as something that excites or scares you. You can see it as something that contributes positively to your performance or negatively.

***Champions see pressure as a privilege -
an opportunity to do something great.***

The best performers and Champions thrive on pressure. They love the bigger moments. They have prepared their minds (and body) to embrace it. In fact, most high performers will tell you they actually need pressure to perform at their best.

I remember listening to an interview with French Formula 1 Driver Esteban Ocon. He was talking about how his best performances only happen when the pressure is on. He mentioned that he thrived under pressure and needed it to perform at his best. Pressure was something that helped him lock in and focus better. He also mentioned that he had no problem with failing if he knew he gave everything he had. He wanted to finish a race knowing in his heart he couldn't have done anything more.

To perform well under pressure, you must first overcome the fear of failure, which is the root of doubt, nervousness, and anxiety. So, how do you deal better with pressure, you ask? Well, like any other skill, you need to practice it. The more you place yourself in pressure situations, the better you will be equipped to handle them. It's like anything else in life, you can't expect to perform well at something if you haven't spent time working on it.

Talent won't help when it comes to dealing with pressure.
It's a mental skill you have to practice.

To perform well under pressure, you must embrace it. Champions love the challenge of testing themselves and getting out of their comfort zones. The best of the best stay uncomfortable.

How you view pressure is 100% a mindset and attitude. Greg Louganis, the 1984 Olympic gold medalist in Diving said: *"When I enter the arena there is a pressure. I can either view that pressure as fear or I can view it as an exciting challenge."*

Build Grit. Fail forwards. Embrace pressure.

Let your hunger for success be greater than your fear of failure.

– Unknown

CHAPTER 11

CONSISTENCY

ast, but by no means least, the most influential and significant factor when it comes to achieving excellence is **consistency**. There is no progress or success without consistency. Successful people aren't geniuses or perfect beings. They've simply found a way to stay disciplined and consistent in their daily habits and routines.

That's why when you are pursuing excellence, it's important to stay committed and consistent in the ten things that require zero talent as mentioned in this book:

1. The Right Attitude

2. Hunger to Succeed

3. Self-Discipline

4. High Work Ethic

5. Strong Self-Belief

6. Focus

7. Coachability

8. Effort
9. Empowering Self-Talk
10. Grit

Why does consistency matter?

Consistency is what transforms average into excellence. Consistency develops resilience, grit and character. It removes all the excuses and procrastination. Consistency is what gives us the confidence to succeed. Step by step, action by action, we build ourselves.

Consistency leads to Confidence.

As an example, let's look at the highest performers in their fields, be it in sports, corporate, or entertainment. Do you think they got to the level they did by just showing up when they felt like it? Of course not! These high performers committed themselves to staying consistent over the longer term, dedicating countless hours towards mastering their craft.

They overcame the highs and the lows. They stayed consistent throughout it all. Even when they became successful, they didn't sit back and feel satisfied. They kept wanting to learn, grow, and improve.

Famed NFL Football coach Bill Belichick said: *"It's not all about talent. It's about dependability, consistency, and being able to improve. If you work hard, you're coachable, and you understand what you need to do, you can improve."*

The best never stop learning.

Having worked with some of the world's best performers, I've discovered the difference between the great, good and average, comes down to this:

- The **average** performers do what's needed **SOME OF THE TIME**

- The **good** performers do what's needed **MOST OF THE TIME**

- The **great** performers do what's needed **ALL THE TIME**

The difference between the average, good and great isn't found in their IQ or skill level. The difference is found in how committed they are to improving, and how consistent they stay over the longer term.

When you focus on doing your best, one day at a time, it's inevitable that you'll get closer to where you want to be. Opportunities will begin to present themselves. It's so easy to get caught up in the idea that success happens overnight. We see star performers on TV or on the sports field, and think they are just lucky or have been blessed with some God-given talents. It's easy for us to think that they were born that way and success came easy to them. This could not be further from the truth.

'Overnight success' takes at least 15-20 years.

The common denominator these high performers have is the discipline to stay consistent over a long period of time. They showed up every day, regardless of whether they felt like it or not. These high performers were willing to overcome multiple failures and endure the monotony of doing the same *boring* thing, every single day, for years.

Consistent repetition is what builds a skill.

Most people think they need innate gifts and talents to excel in something. They quit the moment things get hard. What they don't realize is, in most cases, all they lack is good old-fashioned consistency. They love the idea of greatness until it's time to do what is required.

No one can argue that Tom Brady achieved greatness in his Football career. Maverick Carter, an American Sports Marketing businessman and Media personality said: *"After I watched Tom Brady win the Super Bowl, it made me start to think that the only thing that makes greatness is consistency over a long period of time."*

When you're consistent, you outlast the competition. You keep going while others give up, and eventually, you'll find yourself ahead of the pack.

Consistency is a SUPERPOWER.

Football Coach Jose Mourinho, describes the difference between a good player and a great player: *"I have worked with many players who are up and down in their performance levels. There is a huge difference between a player that keeps consistent and a player that has moments. And that is what makes the difference between a good player and a top player – consistency."*

When you show up each day consistently, and with the right mentality and attitude, you give yourself the best chance of succeeding. It's about doing what others don't want to do. Olympian Michael Phelps said: *"If you want to be the best, you have to do things that other people aren't willing to do."*

Let's face it, you aren't going to wake up every day and feel inspired. Not even Michael Phelps, the greatest Olympian, ever did. Serbian Tennis player Novak Djokovic said: *"If you want to do well in life, then there will be days that are challenging. Some days I'll feel so bad and unmotivated and have a lack of inspiration. You have to overcome that, you know, and it all starts and ends with your mind. You need to get back to asking yourself what is it that you truly want? What's the purpose? When you have clarity on these things it helps set up the routines, the daily goals, the short term goals, the long term goals."*

Excellence is a product of consistency.

The truth is, some days will be good while others will be tougher. The key to winning the day comes down to your attitude. Winning the day doesn't mean that everything will go perfectly. Instead, it's when you have done your best with what you had. When you show up each day consistently, and with the right attitude and mentality, you give yourself the best chance of success.

Consistency is what transforms average into excellence.

With discipline and consistency, nothing can stop you. It's important to remember that you develop grit and resilience on the days that are tougher. Grit isn't built from comfort so the next time you are having a challenging day, remind yourself: *"It's these kinds of days that make me a mentally tougher person."*

Giannis Antetokounmpo is a Greek-Nigerian professional Basketball player for the Milwaukee Bucks of the National Basketball Association. When it came to what it takes to reach the NBA, the 'Greek Freak', as he's known, had this to say: *"It takes more than skills to be great. That's what people don't understand. You can be the most skillful person on earth, and it still won't be enough to reach the NBA."*

Giannis went on to say: *"The NBA is way more about skills or talent, it's about having the consistency. Look at Lebron James, twenty years in the league. When you think about Lebron, you think about consistency over all those years."*

Giannis had this one final thing to say when it came to his talent and abilities: *"I'm not the most skillful player. I don't have the best dribbling skills. I don't have the best shot. The thing that makes me a step further than others is discipline and consistency."*

Skills aren't enough. You need consistency to be great.

A few years back, I remember speaking with a Premiership Rugby Coach based in the UK. I asked him what he looked for in a player. Unsurprisingly, he mentioned having the game skills and competency to play. However, what mattered most to him was consistency in a player's energy and attitude. That went for staff members as well.

He mentioned that he would far prefer to have a player who was going to bring a consistent 8 out of 10 performance each week rather than a player who was a 10 one week and a 3 the next. In his words: *"It's a long season, so I need to be sure that the players I select will display consistent performances on the pitch."*

English Football Manager, Sean Dyche echoed the same words: *"Consistency of performance is essential. You don't have to be exceptional every week but as a minimum, you need to be at a level that, even on a bad day, you get points on the board."*

One of the world's leading experts in communication is Vinh Quang Giang. A Keynote Speaker from Australia with over 3.5 million Instagram followers, Vinh believes when you're starting a new passion, it's important to take really big steps because it gets you motivated. However, to continue the big steps, it's just not sustainable. Therefore, it's all about consistent action. In Vinh's words: *"Consistency beats intensity."*

Success happens when you build the right habits and stay consistent over time. It's about putting in the work that is required every single day. Success is a result of all the small daily efforts repeated.

The only way you see results is when you stay consistent.

NFL Hall of Famer, Tom Brady said: *"To be successful at anything, the truth is you don't have to be special. You just have to be what most people aren't. Consistent, determined, and willing to work for it. No shortcuts."*

Consistency is about the process. It's about winning the daily battle. Champions don't let their feelings override their discipline. They stay consistent in doing what needs to be done.

Aim for progress, not perfection.

Don't make **perfect** the enemy of **good enough**. Remind yourself that doing something is better than nothing. Even finding 20 minutes in your day to exercise is good enough for that day. The main thing is that you do something and keep the habit burning.

Remember that slip ups and mistakes will happen. Failure will occur. That's okay. Life happens. The most important thing is to get back on track as soon as possible. Embrace failure as part of the process.

Consistency doesn't mean perfection. The great American Tennis Coach, Brad Gilbert said: *"The pursuit of perfection doesn't exist. It will only make you miserable."* Consistency means you aim to be reliable. Consistent character is more important than perfection itself and can be learned through practice and repetition. I've been asked many times how I've been able to write eight books in eight years. The answer is actually very simple. Staying consistent. Sitting down and writing regardless of how I feel on the day.

Maintaining the habit of doing what needs to be done is key.

Excellence requires consistency in your attitude, your standards, your habits, your routines and your work ethic. Aristotle said: _"We are what we repeatedly do. Excellence, then, is not an act, but a habit."_

Be consistent in your word. This will lead to trust

Be consistent in your mood. The energy you bring is everything

Be consistent in your routines. Develop winning lifestyle routines

Be consistent in your work ethic. Hard work always pays off

Be consistent in your health. No success happens without it

Be consistent in your habits. Your habits determine your future

If you choose to remain consistent and persistent, great things will eventually happen. The work you've put in will pay off. As best-selling Author Robin Sharma says: *"Consistency is the mother of mastery."*

Day-to-day consistency is what leads to excellence.

Your daily standard of excellence and attitude will determine how far you go. Hollywood Actor, Dwayne Johnson, better known as "The Rock" *said: "Success isn't always about greatness. It's about consistency. Consistent hard work leads to success. Greatness will come."*

Consistency is vital in many areas of life no matter what you do be it business, sports, studies, relationships, fitness, etc. Learning how to commit to changes that benefit you long-term will set you up for success in many areas of your life.

If you are aiming for the top, consistency is the name of the game.

CONSISTENCY WINS.

It's not what you do once in a while that matters.

It's what you do every day.

– Allistair McCaw

CONCLUSION

I'm sure you will agree there are many examples of individuals in this book who have proven that talent is a myth and that if you are willing to commit to the work it takes, you can, and will succeed.

Make the **11 Things That Require Zero Talent** part of your daily routine. Create a vision of who it is you want to become, and then structure a plan to achieve it. Nobody will do it for you. Only you have the power to influence that.

You don't have to be great to start, but you do have to start to be great. Don't waste another day. Procrastination is the thief of time. Life is short and there is nothing worse than regretting what could have been.

With the right attitude and mindset, you can become unstoppable. Aim to create excellence in your daily habits and routines. Stay consistent. Stay patient and learn from your mistakes. Aim for progress, not perfection. Remember that Rome wasn't built in a day, but it was being built daily.

Give up the good for the great. Stay accountable to yourself. You can either make excuses or make progress, but never at the same time. As mentioned throughout this book, a Champion mentality is not about being gifted or talented, it's about being consistent, focused and disciplined.

Greatness awaits you. Excellence is in you. It's time to become the person you were destined to be.

Last but not least, whatever you are pursuing, learn to find joy in the process of becoming. If you are not enjoying the process because your focus is always on the outcome and arriving, that's called stress. Success without fulfillment is the ultimate failure. Many people can be so fixated on the result or outcome that they forget to embrace the moments and the journey. Remember, it's the journey where you will spend the most time, not the destination. **Learn to find joy in the process of becoming.**

SPEAKING & CONSULTING

Alongside his Consulting services, Allistair is also an internationally acclaimed keynote speaker and has spoken in over fifty countries around the globe.

Some topics he speaks on include:
- *Leadership & Coaching*
- *Team & Organizational Culture*
- *Mindset & High Performance*

For speaking enquiries, please e-mail:
info@allistairmccaw.com

FOLLOW ALLISTAIR ON SOCIAL MEDIA!
Twitter: *@allistairmccaw*
Instagram: *@bechampionminded*

YOUR FEEDBACK MATTERS!

Allistair would be so grateful if you could take a few minutes of your time to leave a rating and review on **Amazon**. Your feedback means the world to him! Thank you in advance.

Allistair McCaw

A SPECIAL THANKS TO...

Finally, this book wouldn't have been possible without the editing of Michelle Eyles (ME your VA), and the cover design and layout of Eli 'The Book Guy' Blyden and Jahshua Blyden.

Other Works
by Allistair McCaw